Copyright © 2014 Justin Gilchrist. All Rights Reserved.

No part of this publication can be reproduced or transmitted in any form or by any means, electronic or mechanical, without permission in writing from the author or publisher.

Limit of Liability/Disclaimer of Warranty

While the author has used their best efforts in preparing this book, they make no representations or warranties with respect to the accuracy or completeness of the contents of this book and specifically disclaim any implied warranties of merchantability or fitness for a particular purpose. No warranty may be created or extended by sales representatives or written sales materials. The advice and strategies contained herein may not be suitable for your situation. You should consult with a professional where appropriate. The author shall not be liable for any loss of profit or any other commercial damages, including but not limited to special, incidental, consequential, or other damages.

This book is published in a variety of hard copy and electronic formats. Some content that appears in print may not be available in electronic formats.

www.exitplan.co

To Lesley, TJ and Eve - Thank You.

CONTENTS

Chapter 01 :: This isn't SEO — 6

Chapter 02 :: Debunking Myths — 16

Chapter 03:: Chips on the Table — 22

Chapter 04 :: Starting your Search — 34

Chapter 05 :: With Great Knowledge — 42

Chapter 06 :: When Dinosaurs Roamed the Earth — 54

Chapter 07 :: Portfolio Stars — 70

Chapter 08 :: Do Diligence — 102

Chapter 09 :: Creating Deals — 124

Chapter 10 :: Everyone needs a prenup — 138

Chapter 11 :: After the Honeymoon — 152

01.
THIS ISN'T SEO

11 STAGE 1 - BASIC MONETIZATION

12 STAGE 2 - SEEKING PRODUCT MARKET FIT

13 STAGE 3 - ACQUIRING USERS

14 STAGE 4 - CUSTOMER LIFETIME VALUE

15 STAGE 5 - FULL LIFECYCLE MARKETING

BUSINESS VERSUS MARKETING

The problem with 80% of content that you'll read on blogs, or in yet another generic Kindle book promising you untold riches on the internet, is that it mostly focuses on internet **marketing.**

Rarely, will you find something really worth reading about internet **business.**

Assuming you don't already know, it's important to eventually learn about how to use organic search to attract customers, why Pinterest is a *'totally awesome medium for customer acquisition'* or how changing the color of a button from green to red will increase your revenue 5,000 fold. It's important eventually, but it's not the first thing to fully understand.

What tends to separate the operators and buyers who build big multi-million dollar portfolios from a tiny first purchase, and those that spend years dwelling in the sub $50K per year zone is an understanding of the fundamentals of internet business ... not awesome SEO skills or a *penchant for Facebook Ads*.

I'm assuming you've bought this book knowing at least a little about running a business, however small that might be.

Imagine for a minute you didn't and you were right back at the start of your journey. You have no idea what profit and loss is, no idea how to work with employees or contractors and think 'inventory' is a place scientists go to work.

Imagine this naive version of you was given a restaurant.

You have no employees, no guides or instructions, just all the information in the world on getting customers through the door. What do you think would happen if you managed to fill the restaurant every night? Terrible food, costs that exceeded your turnover and untrained staff would probably be your demise. If you happen to be in a busy tourist area, where repeat business isn't too important, you might just survive. Even if you did though, you would never be a great business that turns over a huge profit year on year.

This is what happens to many buyers and entrepreneurs who fail to ever do something great.

They buy a website, and armed with marketing knowledge, go forward to drive more customers through adverts, SEO or social media. If the business is badly setup and they happen to be average at driving traffic, failure is inevitable. Those visitors that do convert won't be enough thanks to a bad business model.

A badly setup site doesn't always mean failure. If they happen to be an internet marketing prodigy and can drive far more traffic than the people who do this for a living *(the same people who are working for the competition)*, they might make money for a short while. Seeing this first-hand, profits are unlikely to be anything substantial, especially if their cost to acquire one visitor is far greater than what they can earn thanks to a poorly setup business.

If they happen to be a marketing prodigy **and** happen to have bought an outstanding business, then that's as close to a guarantee of success as they'll get. They'll drive a lot of traffic to a business that makes a lot of profit from each visitor.

If you're that prodigy, **and** you're confident you can find an outstanding business, then it's safe to send this book back. For the rest of us, a little theory occasionally goes a long way.

Just like the other theory parts of this guide, understanding Internet Business ownership from a higher level won't just save you time chasing the wrong goals, but it will also help you increase profitability far quicker.

If you're a natural web entrepreneur, these are the things you probably do subconsciously that result in success, regardless of the site or project that you're working on.

If you're not a natural, the good news is that you certainly don't need to be to see the same end results. All of the concepts in this section can be digested in five or ten minutes, but understanding how they work together will have a profound effect on what you're trying to achieve.

Start by remembering that every asset you own or purchase will live in one of the five stages on the next few pages. Those assets closer to the 5th stage tend to be more profitable and reliable businesses than those closer to the 1st stage.

Your job as a buyer is to understand your primary objective at each stage, and to acknowledge where the business you're about to purchase is.

Your job as an owner is to move the business through each stage as quickly as you can whilst maintaining profitability.

When you do, you no longer have a website. You now have an Internet Business. Your priorities should be guided by where you are in this sequence, and whether what you intend to do will move you closer to the next stage.

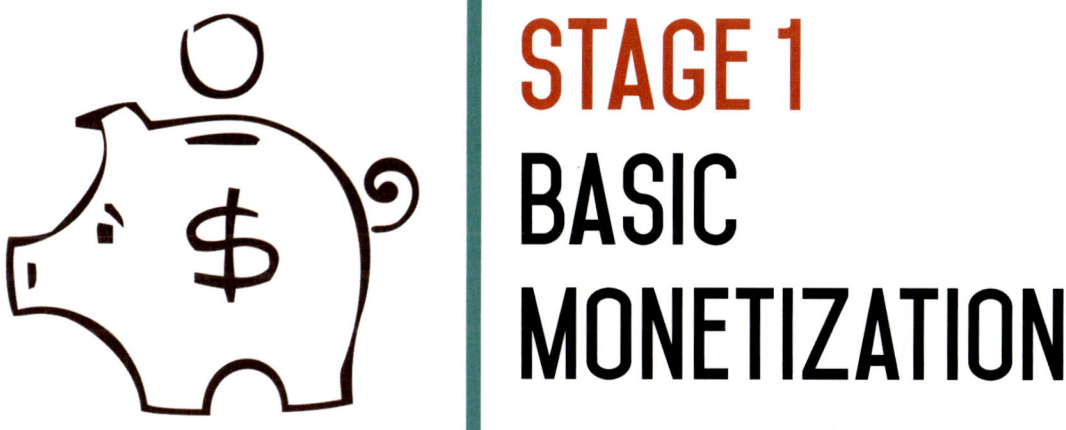

STAGE 1
BASIC MONETIZATION

Revenue per unique user (RPU) gives a crude snapshot of how well a website is monetized. It can be also used as a benchmark when compared to other sites within a similar niche or vertical.

We use revenue rather than profit per user. It allows for comparisons that are unaffected by a site's inefficient operations or high fixed costs. It simply looks at monetization choices and how well visitors convert.

RPU should be one of the first metrics that you track with a new purchase. If the RPU is relatively low compared to other sites in your niche, then you can make improvements with your existing traffic that will most likely generate increased revenue.

If your RPU is already high, then it's usually wise to explore new sources of visitors and new paid traffic channels (like Pay per Click, Paid Social Traffic or buying banner advertisements). Assuming the profit margin on each customer transaction is significant, it's likely you'll have plenty left to fund the cost of paid advertising.

For some models like ecommerce, RPU is a fairly limited benchmark as products can vary massively in price. The amount of revenue that one user can generate from a sofa store for example, will far exceed someone selling flowers online, but the profit involved could be identical. Ideally, you should only use it as a benchmark against other sites with a near identical product portfolio or rather, use **Gross Profit per User** instead.

Once you have an idea of where the site is in terms of RPU, you can move to Stage 2 and start to evaluate your **Product Market Fit**.

STAGE 2
PRODUCT MARKET FIT

Every site has an element of product market fit and achieving the ideal fit is vital before seeking new customers.

A product market fit is usually more concerned with having the right model and monetization choice for the type of audience or vice versa. For example, a site attracting a young audience through online games is unlikely to make an ecommerce strategy work, especially if the average user is too young to own a credit card. Instead, shifting focus to **CPA and Incentivized offers** like competitions and surveys to unlock features is more likely to result in better returns.

Likewise, a site that sells home medical devices and attracts viewers through content about various illnesses and home / herbal remedies is unlikely to convert at a significant rate. While the traffic is in the right niche, and more than likely plentiful (due to high search volume), the intent of the viewer is not to make a purchase, but to immediately solve a problem for themselves. Shifting the traffic profile towards people seeking to monitor and improve their long-term health is more likely to convert at a better rate.

Changing the traffic profile, or increasing the number of visitors within the existing profile, is usually the start of Stage 3 - an established **customer acquisition strategy**.

STAGE 3
ACQUIRING USERS

Almost every site will have sources of new visitors like Organic (from Search Engines), Social or Paid traffic. Each traffic source will convert with varying degrees of effectiveness. Your goal at this stage is to find a sustainable and scalable way of acquiring traffic that converts.

You can tweak the makeup of your traffic profile to increase conversions (the number of people who make a purchase, sign up or view an advert), transactions and profit. But this comes only after you understand what's happening with a site's **RPU** and its **Product Market Fit** in stage 1 and stage 2.

Consider this example. You have a site that sells fashion accessories, many of which are endorsed and worn by celebrities. You receive a lot of traffic from Facebook, but it's mostly from people just wanting to see pictures of movie stars. You receive a lot of visits but they fail to convert because of low relevancy. Instead, you decide to grow referral traffic through guest blogging on highly relevant blogs aimed at people looking for new wardrobe ideas.

If a site has a good **Product Market Fit** and a healthy or above average **RPU**, then you could increase **paid traffic acquisition** as it's both scalable, and most likely affordable.

Underdeveloped sites and rookie owners typically stop here and ignore the next two stages. This is also the imaginary line between purchases that are made for development and revenue growth and those more mature investments that have approached their ceiling but represent a more stable long term purchase (operational plays).

In layman's terms, grown-up sites begin here…

STAGE 4
CUSTOMER LIFETIME VALUE

If a website has historical data (at least 1 year), you can calculate a **customer's lifetime value or CLTV**.

CLTV factors in conversion, monetization and retention and is frequently the deciding value in a site's sophistication. As most growth will come from paid acquisition of some form (technically, even blogging is paid acquisition as there is a time / resource cost associated with it), knowing the CLTV and being able to extend it, means access to more sources of traffic than other competing sites in the same vertical.

For example, sites that monetize traffic through **display advertising**, making no attempt to encourage repeat visits or frequent communication with a visitor will only be able to pay a maximum of what that visitor is worth based on one visit and their total impressions / the chance of one click.

A more sophisticated site would capture that visitor's details and encourage them to return through engaging content delivered via social media and email. They could also sell related products or services to a segment of that list. With tools in place to track that customer's lifetime value, it's more likely that this site could pay far more than what the original site could pay to recruit the same visitor.

The sites with the highest CLTVs are those who can pay more for a customer and still profit. This means they have the widest options for growth and can create their own barrier to entry for new competitors, who more than likely can't compete with the amount they can pay for a new visitor.

An operator can develop and increase their CLTV through **Stage 5 - Full Lifecycle Marketing**.

STAGE 5
FULL LIFECYCLE MARKETING

Most owners understand the concept of monetizing a visitor once, when they have first contact with the site. However, profitability comes from understanding how to monetize each stage of the customer funnel.

For ecommerce sites for example, this might be monetizing checkout confirmation pages with adverts and offers, offering warranties through follow up emails and attracting people who abandon their shopping cart back to the site through retargeting and social media in order to offer them an alternative product.

Each contact with the customer is another opportunity to either build the relationship, generate revenue or where possible both, as one effectively benefits the other.

We're lucky to be in an era where there's an abundance of tools that make lifecycle marketing way easier than it used to be such as InfusionSoft or Drip (getdrip.com). Even email software like Mailchimp has started to implement elements of customer tracking and personalization into its platform.

You should see setting up a well-balanced and profitable funnel as your ultimate priority in creating a business that will deliver lasting value for you as the investor. More so, you create a business with a huge barrier to entry regardless of your niche and one that you can eventually sell for many times more than those businesses left behind at Stage 3

02.
DEBUNKING MYTHS

19   THE AVERAGE MULTIPLE IS ...

20   BUYING AN UNDERVALUED BUSINESS IS THE WAY TO GO

21   GOOD BUSINESSES NEVER HAVE TO PAY FOR TRAFFIC

FORGOT EVERYTHING YOU'VE BEEN TOLD

Even what I may have previously told you in blog posts or guides I've published a number of years ago. The problem we have with any emerging industry is that things move relatively quickly. In the space of three or so years, we've seen a complete overhaul of what's valid in this industry and what isn't.

The underlying principles are still the same - you find a good and possibly undervalued internet business, add value, extract a profit and get a return on your investment.

Everything else seems to have evolved and I'll start by debunking some common myths that were probably true some time ago but aren't true now.

#1 THE AVERAGE MULTIPLE IS...

The sale-price-multiple myth started at 4-6x monthly revenue many years ago and moved to 6 - 8x monthly profit as sites became more sophisticated. Currently, some blogs and articles are reporting that **good** internet businesses sell for 12 - 16x monthly net profit. This is a long way from the truth.

According to data from **BizBuySell** combined with our own data from brokered transactions, the average sale multiple of an internet business above $20K is currently around 2.7x annual net profit. If you're looking for smaller purchases, expect to pay more when it's listed on a public marketplace, as the scarcity of 'good' businesses, combined with lots of competing bidders will always drive prices up for certain listings. Remember that an average multiple is just that. The range of multiples can vary widely from the average depending on both the niche and the site. Businesses sell far above and below the average for a multitude of reasons that we'll cover later on.

The bad news here is that this average continues to increase due to a current imbalance in supply and demand. There's an over-supply of buyers looking for opportunities **under $200K**, and a shortage of good businesses at or below that price.

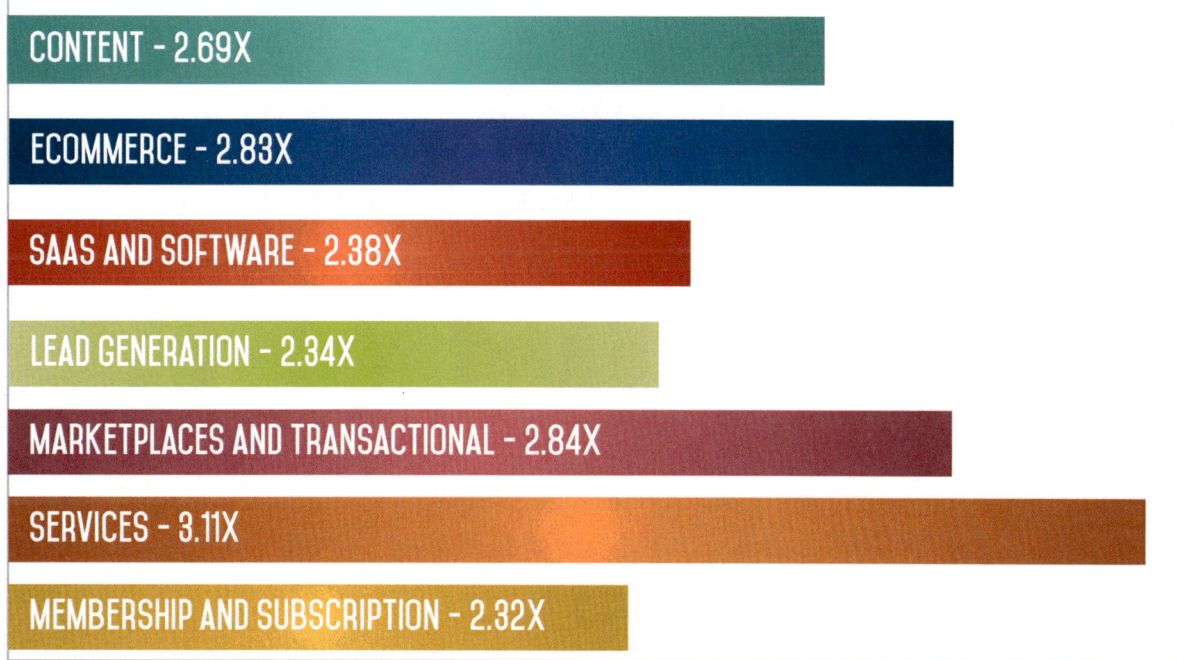

Asking Price to Net Profit Multiple by Category

#2 BUYING AN UNDERVALUED BUSINESS IS THE WAY TO GO

This isn't really a myth ... it's true. Finding an undervalued website is undoubtedly the best way to achieve the highest return on your investment, but your definition of 'undervalued' has to be substantially different from what it would have been in 2010.

Back in times of old, undervalued was finding a site where the owner genuinely had no idea of its value – for example, the 6 year old authority site in the personal finance niche with 250K monthly visits that sold for **$700** (*true story*). Or the established ecommerce site you picked up on a forum for 4x monthly net that you later sold at auction for 1.5x annual net.

It's not that undervalued sites no longer exist; they've just become incredibly scarce. Finding those undervalued gems is near impossible and can often turn out to be a waste of your time and resources.

Today, buyers and sellers are savvier than they've ever been. Combine this with better awareness of where to buy websites, more education for sellers and far more buyers competing for the same deals and we have a situation where the deals actually worth buying are at best, fairly priced.

Now, *'undervalued'* really refers to sites where for example:

1) You have an opportunity to change the monetization and achieve a higher return per user

2) The site could convert X% more users by changing the design to something mobile responsive or

3) The purchase would be a strategic acquisition to complement other similar sites in your portfolio giving you economies of scale.

The reality is that you'll need to pay a *'fair'* price to buy a good business, or spend precious time looking and accepting the risk of your bargain becoming a turkey.

#3 GOOD BUSINESSES NEVER HAVE TO PAY FOR TRAFFIC

The crowd favorite in this industry has always been the simple AdSense site. As well as being easy to operate (more content = more money), operating costs and maintenance for AdSense sites are typically next to nothing. As your traffic will mostly come from search, you have no marketing costs so in some ways it can seem like the ideal business. But then **Experience** comes along and spoils all of your fun.

Experience sure can be a cruel teacher.

Anyone who has seen their visitor count (and revenue) halve overnight after a search algorithm update wiped out their traffic should feel great that they now know better. There are several advantages to paying for your traffic, the most important being

- **Control.** When you pay for traffic you ultimately own and control that traffic source, meaning that it's highly unlikely that it will suddenly change or stop.

- **Scalability.** Growing traffic and hence growing the business through SEO usually involves a painstaking and unpredictable process of link building and content outreach. Scaling a paid traffic campaign is simply a case of research and budget.

- **Cost.** With paid traffic, you not only know the true cost of your marketing expenditure upfront, but you can also directly calculate the cost to acquire one customer. Compare this to spending money and time on SEO / Social media engagement where you often have no idea what equates to what result.

Good businesses are ones that can consistently generate a profit. Great businesses are ones that have a scalable and repeatable system for doing so.

Be prepared to pay more for businesses that already have a profitable campaign in place, or alternatively try to find businesses that rely on organic traffic where similar sites have profitable campaigns in place.

03.
CHIPS ON THE TABLE

25	WHAT WILL $10K GET ME TODAY?
26	IS THERE A MINIMUM BUY-IN SWEET SPOT?
28	A NOTE ON TESTING THE WATER
30	OPERATING CAPITAL
31	PAYING FOR TIME

CHIPS ON THE TABLE

Now we're looking at the practical side of buying internet businesses, it seems like a sensible time to address how much you'll need to make a realistic start.

If you have no intention of spending at least $5,000 please stop reading.

Early on, I sort of made a promise that I intend to keep – I'll make the process of establishing a profitable income stream from buying a website almost guaranteed.

It's not impossible to find an undervalued site where the owner simply doesn't appreciate the true value. It's also not impossible to find a profitable, healthy and established site for less than $5K. It's just unlikely and very, very hard. What I'm here to show you is a relatively predictable way of building a sustainable income.

Chasing the illusive $2K bargain just isn't a dependable enough strategy, because there are too many ways it can fail.

Finding a good-enough purchase at even $10K isn't fool proof. Actually, it's quite difficult to do without being incredibly creative, but it's also a fairly safe assumption that you will be able to make it happen within 2 – 8 weeks of looking.

The main problem, is that for every dollar below the minimum sweet spot (more below), quality seems to drop exponentially. Also, competition for that same site increases, making it both harder to find and relatively more expensive to buy.

WHAT WILL $10K GET ME TODAY?

On a relatively high valuation of around **3x annual net** for a small but established and healthy site, you should be able to find something that

- Has at least 3 years history and generates approximately $270 monthly net

- Most likely uses contextual advertising as its primary source of revenue but may also have product / affiliate sales

- Has a mailing list, an active social presence and receives around 55% of traffic from organic search

- Has fairly low maintenance requirements outside of creating content

On a slightly more average valuation at this price range of around **1.8x annual net**, you're more likely to buy a site that

- Has 1 - 2 years history and generates approximately $460 monthly net

- Relies wholly on contextual advertising for revenue

- Requires frequent content updates or moderation

- Receives around 70% + of traffic from Organic Search

It's important to know that these aren't target criteria; it's simply what is typical at that price range. If you can find a 9 year old site with a profitable paid campaign in place, and various elements of full-funnel monetization, then bite the seller's hand off to get the deal!

The minimum sweet spot

The sweet spot for the absolute minimum you should spend to get started could be the point where valuations are lowest and the number of competing buyers is lowest too. To get a crude idea where this point is, we can look at data from **Flippa.com** - the world's largest marketplace for selling websites.

Even if Flippa is not the place you'll eventually shop at, it shows the number of bidders (*i.e. interested parties*) on a site – something we can't see with information from brokered private listings. We need to appreciate that any data we look at will be useless over $100K, as this is where most Flippa listings stop. Also in some cases, the data could be skewed by anomalies.

The idea is with enough sold listings to work with, looking at averages should 'smooth' out the inevitable bits of bad data. We also removed any listing that was relisted or listed more than once, as it was assumed that the first listing couldn't be relied upon.

The takeaway here is to use this as inspiration – not gospel, or rigorous scientific research.

When we look at the number of bids against price, it shows the number of competing bidders generally decreases when the price of the business goes up – no new revelations here.

WEBSITE SELLING PRICE	AVERAGE NUMBER OF BIDDERS
$10K - $15K	43
$16K - $25K	35
$26K - $35K	56
$36K - $50K	37
$51K +	31

It follows the logic that there are fewer bidders at higher capital requirements; i.e. less people have more money to spend.

What's interesting is that the most competitive category above $10K isn't **$10k - $15K**, but **$26K - $35K** where I guess you tend to find more sites that surpass $1K in monthly income without being out of the price range of the majority of + $10K buyers who frequent Flippa.

When we look at sale price multiples versus selling price, it seems the sweet spot is between $36K and $50K – the bracket that tends to sell for the lowest valuations.

WEBSITE SELLING PRICE	AVERAGE SALE MULTIPLE *
$10K - $15K	1.86 x
$16K - $25K	1.29 x
$26K - $35K	1.44 x
$36K - $50K	1.12 x
$51K +	1.30 x

Sales multiples quoted are multiples of annual net profit

Truthfully, I've no idea why this is.

On the one hand, it could be down to bad data or maybe not enough data for sites at this price range to give us a meaningful average. On the other hand though, it ties in with the amount of activity at each price bracket. Where you have more bidders in an open marketplace, you inevitably have more bids and hence a higher selling price.

This would explain why sites between $10K and $15K have the highest average valuations on auction sites. On the upper end, there tends to be a distinct lack of quality listings at the + $36K range, with the majority of these types of sites now being sold privately, through Flippa's private service or through brokers.

The sites that sold at public auction and hence the only ones included in this dataset were in my opinion, quite poor quality sites. These were possibly the ones that brokers avoided, so it makes sense that this group had low valuations.

There's also the unspoken understanding that '*serious*' buyers tend to avoid public auctions thanks to an excess of poor quality listings. Even the better listings at higher price points attract fewer bids.

The 'second sweetest' spot of **$16K - $25K** also happens to be the twilight zone for most brokers. This is the price at which it's borderline whether or not there would be enough commission in the deal to make it worthwhile. This can force many sellers towards the auction option which again, isn't the most suitable choice.

A NOTE ON TESTING THE WATER

In any given working month, I'll speak to several first-time website buyers every week.

Approximately half have the idea that they should test the water first before buying a serious purchase and choose to do so with $1K - $5K. The logic is to see if they can get the idea to work before committing a larger amount.

Although the logic makes sense, this always turns out to be an epically bad idea. Take this example.

You know a little about running restaurants and decide to buy one that's up for sale for $250K, located on a busy intersection.

The price is significantly higher than other restaurants in the same area, but it has a good location, excellent staff and a great reputation. Profits have also been increasing year on year.

If the restaurant is as good as it's slightly overpriced valuation would lead you to believe, then running an operation like this should be relatively straightforward, as most of the components to support and deliver growth are already in place.

You decide that before committing your life savings you should test the water on something smaller for a few months, just to make sure everything works as you're being told it should do. You decide to buy a restaurant in a neighborhood where the brown bags are for malted goods - not Macy's, at the bargain price of $5K.

What do you think your chances of success are with the $5K restaurant?

Even Gordon Ramsay would struggle with a business that lacks the right components, so as a first time operator you'll find it near impossible. I've deliberately used a retail business as it's something most of us can instantly relate to.

The problem seems to be when people think of internet businesses as anything less than offline businesses that require the same amount of attention, thought and in some cases, resources.

Go back to the example of buying a $1,000 site first to test the water and what will usually happen is:

- There are lots of improvements that need to be made so you throw good money and time after bad.

- There's no scalable system for finding new visitors or customers, so you endlessly trade time for clicks. (Either time in doing or time in managing those that are doing for you). The results are less than impressive.

- If you do make an improvement it's marginal and unlikely to motivate you. Assuming your $1,000 site does $100 monthly and you deliver a 40% increase in monthly turnover, you're now earning $140. **All it took to get there was four months of hard work**.

- That lack of redundancy you get with buying a $1K business comes back with a vengeance. There's a search algorithm update and you lose half of your traffic overnight. That, and eight or so months of putting the majority of your free time into this test project.

What started out as a fun experiment leaves you resenting yet another lost weekend or evening.

At this point, most people get so side-tracked they give up on the bigger dream and decide that if they can't make it work on a smaller site, they'll probably fail with a larger one and decide not to proceed.

Even the shrewdest operators I know out there would struggle to make a success of a $1K site, so it's highly unlikely that someone starting out for the first time will be able to make it all happen.

Test the water by working on, or for a site with a similar size to what you intend to purchase but avoid buying a cheap deal at all costs. Basing your decision to proceed on the outcome of an impossible challenge is a sure-fire way to mislead yourself into failure.

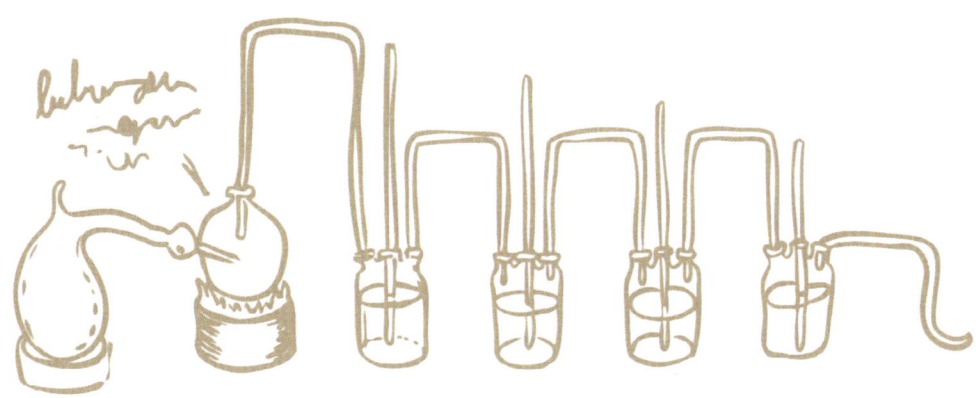

OPERATING CAPITAL

It's debatable whether you'll need to reserve some cash for operating capital.

When you're at the reins of a new site, it's likely that your creative juices start flowing with fresh ideas. This is the time you need to capitalize on that enthusiasm, as time tends to erode passion.

> *Six months in, you'll find it a lot harder to be motivated enough to implement that new sales funnel, or to experiment with a new website design.*

Setting aside operating capital makes it easier to get things done quickly without having the bottleneck of your own time stand in the way. In some cases, I've used cash-flow from the site to fund operating requirements, but you'll often find that you need a little more to get the larger initial projects done properly.

From my own experience these typically include:

- **Hiring a front end or web interface designer** to make changes to landing pages or implement better opt-in forms (tip – don't hire developers or coders for front end work. Hire a 'front end developer' or specialist User Interface designer that can also code – there's a huge difference in both the quality and the amount of time they'll take to complete the job).

- **Paying an affiliate manager** to find and manage affiliates on your behalf to promote a site's product (tip #2 – setting up an affiliate WONT get you sales. The hard work is in the promotion of your program to those affiliates to motivate them to sell).

- **Hiring a developer** to fix minor bugs or annoyances or to deal with the backlog of feature updates.

- **Making a site mobile responsive** so you provide people viewing on mobile devices a better user experience.

- **Setting up funnel management software** like InfusionSoft.

- **Paying an SEO agency** to remove a ton of bad links that were built by the previous owner in 2007 and have since turned toxic.

Assuming you've spent time and money taking the risk out of the purchase with good due diligence, now wouldn't be a good time to see all that go to waste by hiring semi competent cheap contractors to do the work on your site.

I don't believe in overpaying, but you're looking for a margin of safety. The new site is still an unknown entity to you, and hiring smart people who charge a fair price for what they do can sometimes mean the difference between success and failure overall.

I've been moved to tears watching people spend over $250K on a site, and then choose an unreliable halfwit to code some new features, all because their Elance bid was $600 cheaper than the more credible alternative.

Set aside a realistic budget from the start and never be afraid to pay for quality work.

Paying for Time

When you start to look at the more sophisticated sites on sale, you'll hopefully adopt the same grudge that anyone who does due diligence on a regular basis tends to share.

Sellers are rarely realistic about their fixed costs, the most common problem being the failure to put a value on the time they spend in the business themselves.

For even the most basic site, you will always need two things if you choose to grow or even just maintain your current position:

a) Content, Moderation or Development

Most sites require content of some kind, even if it's adding new inventory for an ecommerce store. The exceptions are sites that have user-generated content such as forums or social sites, but then you require moderation.

SaaS products may not require content, but they do require development and ongoing fixes. Occasionally, you may find a good ecommerce business that relies on just a few limited products, and as such, doesn't require any additional content to grow or function.

b) Marketing and Promotion

This could be content for marketing (like social media updates or guest blogging), or possibly paid advertising management.

Ideally, once the site is generating enough cash flow to pay for it, you'll hire people to take care of these two areas for you. However, unless the business you're acquiring already has this in place, hiring the same day you acquire the site may not be the best idea. It's sort of like adopting a grown child then leaving that child with a (*bad chain-smoking*) nanny for the first six months when you should be getting to know each other.

Firstly, there's the question of knowledge.

Fundamentally, all AdSense sites, Forums or Ecommerce stores are the same, but every site has idiosyncrasies related to its unique blend of audience and content. You need to work with that site for a short while to really understand it. Without understanding what you're delegating, outsourcing the most critical tasks of a business that you've just acquired is likely to result in problems.

Outside of just knowledge, it's also about cost.

Keeping your costs down to a minimum is crucial when you're just getting started. You will make mistakes and you will need all the cash you have to stay in the game.

In fact, a key difference between those who succeed doing this and those who don't tends to be persistence.

Sometimes, you'll make a great purchase but something will go wrong several months or even years in. Providing you've conducted good due diligence, this won't be too severe. It's usually something you can fix, but you'll still need to account for that likely interruption to cash flow while you're putting things right.

Rarely, will you make a perfect purchase first time round.

If you're already $xx,xxx in the hole after the purchase, having twice that spend in monthly costs after you've hired a crack team of outsourced workers, is likely to be the kick in the teeth that keeps you down. That, and the skepticism from your caring other half, who wants you to stop wasting money and take that consulting offer you had after leaving your job.

You can't get back what you've spent on the site itself, but having money in the bank (rather than spending on it on the wrong people or things) will often buy you the runway you need to keep going and iron out those inevitable problems.

The exception is hiring for one off tasks that need to be completed in first few weeks of the acquisition. This is the time when you'll need expert help the most, so spending some capital to reduce your workload is a wise idea. The issue is when you continue to rely on that help, without ever really understanding the work that is being completed on your behalf.

Eventually, your goal should absolutely be to outsource everything that doesn't require you to complete it personally, but in the interim budget time as well as money to get to know your new purchase inside out.

04.
STARTING YOUR SEARCH

36 BROKERS AND AGENCIES

37 FORUMS

39 MARKETPLACES AND CLASSIFIEDS

39 BUY SIDE BROKERS AND LEAD GENERATION SERVICES

40 THE WORST WAY TO SPEND YOUR WEEKEND

STARTING YOUR SEARCH

Brokers and Agencies

The last few years have seen the emergence of specialist internet-only brokers.

Brokers make money when they sell a site on behalf of a client, and charge the seller a fee based on the value of the sale. This is typically 8 – 12% but can be as high as 15% on smaller sites and as low as 6% on much larger ones.

Apparently, these poor unpaid brokers have to work relatively hard for their money; each deal involves spending time with the client, dealing with numerous prospective buyers, preparing sales brochures, handling agreements etc. The 8% - 12% commission will have to equate to something that makes their time worthwhile, and so it's unlikely to find a brokered business for sale at less than $20K.

The biggest advantage to buying through a broker is probably the time saving. It's usually safe to assume that most of the lower quality listings will have been filtered out. The options that you'll find available have usually had some basic security checks conducted. This mean the seller is less likely to be a fraudster, or someone that will inevitably disappear with your money, but it's still not unheard of.

I use words like 'usually' and 'less likely' because brokers are far from being a sure thing.

You should always bear in mind that a broker in a buy transaction works for the seller, so you will always need your own representation in the form of Due Diligence and Legal Advice.

In doing client due diligence at Centurica, some of our lowest scoring sites have been listings represented by individuals calling themselves brokers. There are no legal requirements or licenses to be an internet business broker.

You will need to apply a certain amount of due diligence to the brokerage themselves, if they are someone you've never done business with.

Even the most trusted agencies occasionally miss things, which can make a business that seems perfect on the surface, a nightmare a few months after you've bought it. Never trust someone who advises you to skip either of these stages. It may be a deal killer for them, but it's a life saver for you if something happens to be wrong with the asset you're about to purchase.

The downside to buying from a broker is price. It's in the broker's best interest to get the highest price they can for their client, so at best you'll pay a fair price and at worst you'll pay more. Just like when you buy advertising, there is always room for negotiation on price, or on terms.

How much negotiation depends on how many interested parties a listing has, so use the amount of time a listing has been on the market as guide to how much you expect. The typical discount between the asking and selling price is around **10% - 15%**.

You can find up to date listings from a wide selection of internet brokers at **centurica.com/marketwatch**.

Forums

It's possible to find a good purchase on a forum, but so is finding a contact lens in a haystack.

There's a small chance it will happen, but that chance is so small it makes looking a waste of your time and resource. If you happen to come across a good opportunity on a forum then grab it with both hands, but it's most likely not worth wasting your time searching on a regular basis.

The world's largest website marketplace came from forum beginnings, but it became the largest marketplace by making a transition. The open nature of forums means almost anyone can post, while inexperienced volunteers moderate. As a buyer, trying to decipher between high quality listings and low quality scams takes processing time which is better spent on looking in higher quality places.

The Wisdom of Crowds
Forums can still be a good place to meet potential sellers and to find like minded entrepreneurs. I've met some great, experienced people on forums but with the good also comes the bad.

Large forums dedicated to internet marketing tend to attract a high number of timewasters and dishonest sellers who find safety hiding behind their avatar.

THE ASS IN A LION'S SKIN.

Forums exclusively around the topic of buying and selling internet businesses are often very small, with a maximum of 10 – 15 active posters at any one time. Usually, 80% of posts will be from just two or three individuals (moderators and owners) so the usefulness of that forum comes down to their personal experience and agenda.

The best options that combine volume with relevant subject matter tend to be those around a specific niche, with an area for buying and selling websites such as hosting or affiliate forums. If you do choose to spend time on a forum, choose one with a large enough community so that bad advice or opinions posing as fact are always questioned and filtered out.

The people who run and moderate small forums in the online business sector are usually happy to provide free advice. This can be an excellent resource for smaller purchases, but dangerous if you're spending more than $10K on a website. I'd always rather pay for advice when a large sum is on the line, and rely on the wisdom of a professional, who wouldn't be in business if they ever gave bad advice.

It's the same reason why you would probably never take legal or serious medical advice from a forum, even though that advice costs money elsewhere.

Marketplaces and Classifieds

Currently, there are only a handful of marketplaces that are worth mentioning, with **Freemarket.com** currently receiving a lot of attention.

If you're looking at spending less than $20k, then a marketplace is probably your most predictable bet. The upside is that you can sometimes find something that has been listed unprofessionally, but contains a lot of hidden value waiting to be realized and sells for much less than it should.

The downside, especially with marketplaces that have no listing criteria, is that you will inevitably have to sort through many poor quality sites in order to find a deal worth buying.

Classifieds tend to offer a mix of listings from brokers and listings from private sellers, so finding an undervalued deal is rare. Interestingly, you often tend to find a higher percentage of 'serious' listings in un-moderated classifieds, than you would typically find in a marketplace. Currently **BizBuySell.com** seems to lead the way for Internet Business classifieds.

Buy Side Brokers and Lead Generation Services

A relatively new option, but one that's gaining traction is to use a company that will generate leads for you. These are vetted to match your buying criteria and pre-filtered to remove poor quality sites.

Due to the sheer amount of manual work involved, this is really only suitable for purchases over $250K.

The advantage is that you get assistance on every part of the sale process. Many buy-side brokers will offer help with Due Diligence, non-legal reviews of contracts and terms of sale, in addition to advising on the transfer to ensure the sale goes ahead without a glitch.

THE WORST WAY TO SPEND YOUR WEEKEND

All of the previously mentioned sellers of websites and internet businesses for sale share a common theme. They are people who have realized the need to sell, most likely done some research, and actively promoted the sale of their business.

There's a theory that the best businesses are bought - not sold. Therefore, being pro-active and finding websites to buy that have not yet been listed, is a way to find bargains below value. That's technically true, but as with everything on the web, not so straightforward.

The standard route to finding non listed deals is to send cold emails to owners of sites that loosely fit your criteria. You can find the email address for the owners of most sites through a little searching on the site itself, looking at the site's WHOIS record, or using prospecting tools like Buzzstream.com.

Something about this approach always reminds me of mining for bitcoin. There's big potential in doing this, and a few success stories floating around the web, but I'm yet to meet someone who does this as a full time repeatable and scalable business process.

The idea is to send a site owner an email asking if they would consider selling their site. By going direct to an owner rather than approaching someone who has already shopped around, or has to factor in 10% for broker fees, you should theoretically get a better deal.

The theory is simple, and the idea works. I've made it work successfully on a few occasions and bought good sites as a result, but there's a major problem. **It's seriously hard work for relatively little reward.**

From my experience doing this in early 2013 (using a semi-automated approach)

- 75% don't reply to your email or your email goes to spam

- 10% reply with a 'thanks but no thanks'

- 10% reply positively, but only to find out how much someone would be willing to pay with no intention of ever selling unless the valuation was 1 birrion dorrars

- 3% will sell, but only at a valuation that's way above what you're prepared to pay

- 1.6% will sell at a fair price

- 0.4% will sell below market value

These are the percentages to get to an agreement, not a completed deal. Less than 50% of all people who agree to sell, actually complete. After you've made your offer, the seller will usually shop around once they know you're interested. Thanks to all the success stories from the valley, people hear the words acquisition and immediately think Facebook money. The chances are, they will contact a broker who will tell the seller they can get far more money with their representation.

You would need to send at least 1,000 emails to stand a chance at buying 1 undervalued business.

This is a good indicator as to how rapidly things change in this industry.

As recently as 2011, the percentages you see above for finding people who would sell at or below market price was almost four times as high. This used to be a worthwhile use of your time, especially if you outsourced the grunt work. As awareness increased and people's tolerance of email spam decreased, this is no longer as effective.

Like most bad ideas being floated in this industry, it's not impossible to do, but most good people will give up way before they hit 100 cold emails sent. Personally, I think there are better ways to spend your Friday night, that don't involve shooting the breeze with the owner of *another-viral-site-of-cats-playing-piano.com*, explaining why her 6 month old site is actually not worth 700 hundred thousand dollars.

It's worth noting that these figures could be marginally better if you went through the effort of heavily personalizing each individual email - I didn't, but doing this en-mass can be soul destroying unless you find a way to systemize, outsource or automate it.

05.
WITH GREAT KNOWLEDGE

46 INTRODUCING THE TRAFFIC LIGHTS

48 THE PRIMARY MODEL

49 AGE

51 THE NICHE OR VERTICAL

52 SITES WITH NO REVENUE

53 DOMAIN VALUE

Knowing the smartest purchases to make is a difficult task.

Internet Businesses are complex entities, so being able to simply run off a list of good types of site is somewhere between insane and impossible. Every site is individual in the way that no two businesses could ever be the same.

Also, every buyer or investor is individual too, so what makes a good purchase for one person could be terrible for another. Outside of financial performance, there are several factors that can determine a 'good' and 'bad' investment but it's only good or bad relative to your strategy.

Outside of the financials, bricks and mortar companies are judged by factors like their industry, location and their staff. Online businesses have their own set of criteria by which the potential value to an investor can be assessed too.

In order to assess each individual purchase opportunity and compare it to others, we need to be able to dissect and categorize each site into components that each carries its own weightings, advantages and disadvantages. Together, these qualities help us take an analytical look at each opportunity from a greater perspective than just doing due diligence allows. The end result is a system you can use to predictably make good purchases.

Whenever I consult and need to explain the concept quickly to a client, it's easiest to think of the system as a jigsaw.

The more pieces you have, the clearer the picture will be as to how the business will eventually look. Sometimes, you might have all the pieces, but still dislike the picture itself. That's your personal preference which is essential to have, but you need an understanding of why you like or dislike a picture (i.e. business) first.

Every potential purchase is made up of at least three segments

- The Primary Model
- Age
- The Niche

The idea is to create your own system where you know the value of each segment before you start searching for an acquisition. For example, perfection in the Age section for one investor may be a 10 year old site, but for you it might be 5 years and above.

It's also worth noting that achieving perfection in these three segments is **not** a replacement for due diligence.

For example, a site can have lots of traffic from visits in a good niche, but if those visitors are mostly from a country where I would struggle to find products or advertisers, then I would avoid the site. This is the kind of information that you will only establish in the due diligence process which we will look at later on.

The idea behind the segments is that it allows you to take a quick snapshot of a business and assess whether it's worth going forward, before investing time or money in the due diligence stage. My own criteria is mostly based on trial and error with different variations across each of the segments, coupled with shared experience from other investors and general common-sense best practice.

If you don't already have a clear or working strategy for making purchases, then the one that follows will safely guide you from buying your first site, to building a relatively low risk portfolio. As your experience grows, you can eventually tweak parts of this to make it your own.

One of the major advantages of using this system is that you can delegate or outsource the task of searching for an acquisition, effectively saving you time. By systemizing the filtering of purchases that don't make a good fit, you can hire a virtual assistant on Elance or Guru to monitor several sources and only send through those opportunities that will potentially work. This will inevitably save you valuable time to focus on doing the right deal.

INTRODUCING THE TRAFFIC LIGHTS

In some of the segments, we look at factors in terms of **Green, Red** and **Amber Lights**.

The idea is, if an opportunity has a **red light** in any area, you pass on it straight away without question or discussion.

Having the discipline to do this saves hours over time.

If an opportunity has all **green lights**, then it's usually wise to proceed by looking at more in-depth information (for example, signing an NDA or requesting a brochure from the broker / seller).

If an opportunity has both **green** and **amber lights**, you can analyze just the **amber** areas before deciding whether you personally are comfortable with this aspect and whether or not you want to proceed.

GREEN LIGHT

Qualities that are highly attractive based on our investment criteria (formed from prior knowledge and experience).

AMBER LIGHT

Qualities that require further verification or are contingent on other factors..

RED LIGHT

Qualities that are unattractive or carry a certain amount of risk based on our investment criteria (formed from prior knowledge, experience and recent external changes and events).

THE PRIMARY MODEL

In layman's terms, the primary model is the main reason for a visitor to engage with the site.

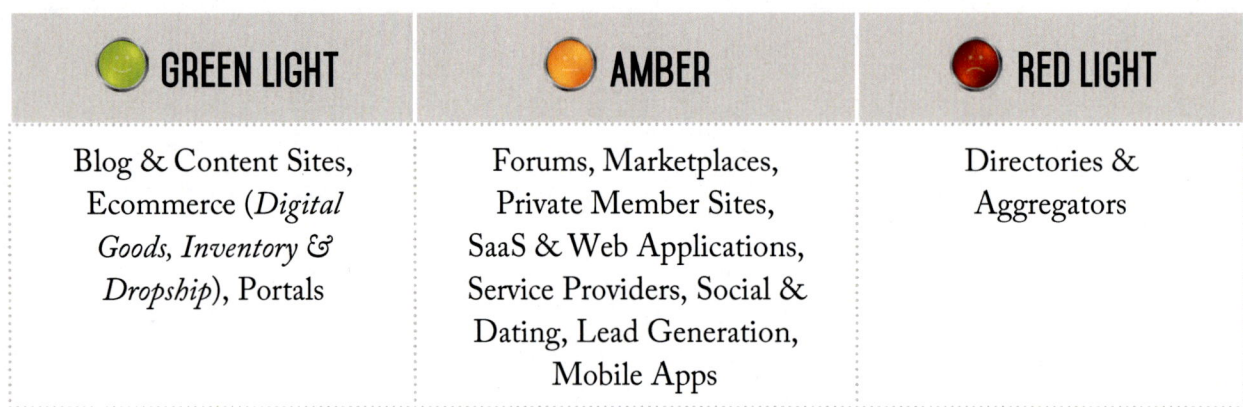

🟢 GREEN LIGHT	🟠 AMBER	🔴 RED LIGHT
Blog & Content Sites, Ecommerce (*Digital Goods, Inventory & Dropship*), Portals	Forums, Marketplaces, Private Member Sites, SaaS & Web Applications, Service Providers, Social & Dating, Lead Generation, Mobile Apps	Directories & Aggregators

Green Light models are highly attractive from an investment perspective because they:

- Are incredibly liquid and in high demand, which means strong resell values and a relatively easy exit.

- Have little to no requirement for specialist knowledge or technical expertise.

- Generally have low resource requirements relative to their turnover. The exception is Ecommerce sites that warehouse a significant proportion of their inventory, rather than ones that drop-ship.

Amber models will generally require more verification due to:

- Forums having high impressions and low click-through rates, few options for monetization and a constant requirement for moderation.

- Marketplaces, Social & Dating and Private member site success being heavily dependent on reaching critical mass, the quality of user engagement and the rate of new customer acquisition.

- SaaS, Mobile and Web Applications requiring technical assessment of the product and its code, in addition to user engagement and retention analysis.

- Lead Generation sites requiring a fluid market of potential lead buyers willing to pay a price that makes selling a lead profitable.

Red Light models should generally be avoided, mostly due to

- Few repeat visits resulting in low customer lifetime value. This limits customer acquisition to methods such as social and organic and makes paid acquisition near impossible.

- Difficult organic user acquisition thanks to Google's frequent changes against sites that aggregate, reuse or repurpose content. Most of these sites fail to achieve an RPU that allows them to profitably buy traffic, leaving them stuck between a rock and a hard place.

A site may fall into 'red' despite being a good solid business.

For example, a directory site with in depth reviews and unique user generated content. This concept is designed to save you time overall by passing on the long-shots. The good opportunities you do come across will more than outweigh the rare (<5%) opportunities that you miss.

AGE

The good news is this section will be incredibly short. I could probably sum it up in one line.

Stay Away From Young Sites

There are exceptions.

Maybe you're buying to save time in building an identical site yourself. Maybe, the business behind the site doesn't matter. If that's the case, ignore this advice. Otherwise, I would class any site under 12 months as a red light, and avoid it all costs.

Ideally, a green light purchase should have **at least 3 years of history** to be considered stable and reliable, whilst 1 – 3 years falls into amber. It may be fine to proceed, but only if you have evidence of strong performance during that time.

When you buy an established site, a fair amount of your cash goes towards buying history and that's important for two reasons.

If the site generates revenue, then older sites are usually more of a guarantee that the revenue is stable.

For example, a site that has seen $3,000 monthly AdSense pay-outs for the last year is far more likely to have a sustainable way of doing this than one that is four months old and has only recently hit that peak in revenue.

In fact, a four month old site generating $3K of AdSense Revenue is, in my opinion, **90% likely to be a short lived opportunity, and one that will eventually die off**, or be banned completely for doing something that Google doesn't quite trust.

There is also the issue with search traffic. Assuming your site relies on at least some search traffic (*which over 80% of sites do*), then a site under 12 months old is still likely to be in Google's metaphorical sandbox – the testing ground for new sites where technically, anything can happen.

New sites tend to receive no search traffic in the first 3 months, followed by an abnormally high amount in months 3 – 9 (especially if the owner knows how to game the system). Unfortunately, rookie buyers will take over a site at month 6 for example, and then a few months later end up with buyer's remorse when their traffic halves and they're left with the realization that the surge in visits was just temporary.

New sites tend to be trouble whilst aged sites are usually worth more for several reasons, stability, proof of concept and aged backlinks being just a few.

THE NICHE OR VERTICAL

The following is not an exhaustive list of niches, however it does cover the majority occupied by websites and internet business typically available for sale.

🟢 GREEN LIGHT	🟠 AMBER	🔴 RED LIGHT
Finance, Healthcare, Employment, Education, Property, Travel Internet Services	Business, Marketing, Cars & Motors, Beauty, Entertainment, News, Family, Sport Home & Leisure, Romance, Fashion, Internet Marketing & MMO, Social Media	Adult, Technology, Consumer Electronics, Copyrighted Downloads or Streaming, Video Games

Green Light Niches tend to be those that typically have a large number of competing corporate advertisers with a substantial budget, resulting in high RPUs across the niche. These also tend to be niches where a wider variety of monetization options exist alongside traditional sources such as display advertising.

Red Light Niches are those where attracting advertisers can be difficult due to the nature of the product / content on offer or where legal action is frequently a possibility and something that could affect the operation of the business. This also extends to niches where there are few monetization options or difficulties in establishing authority.

Amber Niches tend to work well for some buyers, especially those who have prior experience or other sites in the niche, but on whole can be problematic if you're new to that niche / industry.

SITES WITH NO REVENUE

People seem skeptical about buying sites that have no revenue. Rather, new buyers tend to avoid paying a 'good' price for sites that have no revenue but this can sometimes be a short-sighted strategy.

Some of the largest and most profitable content sites that I've come across were built on domains that the owners purchased for their content and age that at the time had no revenue. Today, it's rare that you'll find a site that is totally un-monetized (is that a word yet?). AdSense makes it easy for content creators to quickly get a revenue stream without having to think or put effort into the process.

This can lead to questions about sites that are being sold with no revenue claimed. It's not uncommon for a seller to try something out and realize that it doesn't work, possibly because of their poor implementation, or maybe because of the site's poor traffic quality. Instead of listing the site with revenue and have buyers value it on that alone, they prefer to list it as having *"never being monetized because I didn't have the time"* in the hope people will value it on potential instead.

Knowing the deals that are genuine untapped opportunities is often a case of analyzing everything but the revenue and making sure it's a perfect fit.

This would typically mean finding a site that

- Operates a **green light model**. With no revenue, you will typically be limited to Content sites and Portals.

- Is at least 2 - 3 years old, but preferably much older.

- Has content and traffic in a good, green light niche like finance or education

- Has good quality traffic with high engagement from countries where advertisers typically pay a higher amount per impression. This traffic should also be from a variety of different sources like search, social and referrals.

Deciding how much to pay is a case of looking at what other sites with similar attributes generate and discounting it for the fact that you are not, in this instance, paying for anything that's proven.

For example, if you find an aged blog on personal finance and pensions, you can check what the typical RPU is by looking at other sites for sale in the personal finance niche. Alternatively, you could cheat and look up the RPU on **MonetizationLab.net**. Assuming the RPU is around $0.30, you know it's not unrealistic to assume that monetized in the same way as the 'average' finance site, each unique visitor could earn around $0.30 monthly, so you can multiply up to get an idea of monthly revenue once established.

Naturally, the amount you pay will usually be much less than what you would pay if the site was already monetized. That's your upside as a buyer to have.

DOMAIN VALUE

Domains were not listed as one of the segments that you should assess a potential purchase by, mostly because I personally believe domains no longer matter.

Ten years ago, keyword domains were all the rage. People would search for 'red widgets' for example, and the owner of red-widgets.com would most likely come up first in any search engine's results. All the free traffic they would receive made that domain extremely valuable not just for getting visits, but also for defending against competition.

Situations have changed as they inevitably do in tech. Red-widgets.com is just as likely to rank as widgets-of-another-color.com or even fakeword.ly, as other factors such as age, backlinks and social signals play a much bigger part than the domain itself. Also, sites are now receiving traffic from a much wider variety of sources other than search, with social media sometimes replacing search traffic in its entirety.

In fact, each major Google algorithm change that looks at on-site related factors (the Panda updates) seems to move further away from the importance of the domain. Sites that used to receive a lot traffic for their exact match domain are more and more likely to be penalized in future updates, if there is nothing else about the site to rely on.

In my opinion, this makes paying extra for a premium domain (as part of a website purchase) a short sighted strategy.

The exception is where a domain is great for branding, or where the site receives a lot of type in traffic – books.com or holidays.co.uk for example. This becomes valuable in sectors where the visitor profile tends to be older, or less experienced with the internet and typically doesn't know the difference between an address bar and a search field … **Mom, this is my dedication to you.**

06.
WHEN DINOSAURS ROAMED THE EARTH

58	VALUE VERSUS VALUATIONS
61	THE NON-THEORY PART YOU'VE POSSIBLY SKIPPED AHEAD TO READ
65	DECIDING HOW MUCH TO PAY

BACK IN THE OLD COUNTRY ...

Throughout this book, I'll sometimes use the word 'websites' where in other places I use 'Internet businesses'.

The two are mostly interchangeable, and I use them to refer to the kind of asset I assume we're mostly interested in – established websites generating enough profit, or with enough value to justify a price tag above $20K. In other words, websites that are part of a profitable Internet business. It's relevant to how the current idea of valuing an Internet business is, for want of a more technical term - totally messed up. If anyone tells you there's a correct way to value a website or Internet business, they're either naive or lying; I'll try and explain why.

Established and larger companies are often valued using one of several methodologies, with discounted cash flow possibly being the most common. Theoretically, we should be able to apply this to the smaller internet companies that we're trying to acquire. If you were paying someone to complete a valuation for you, it's probably what you would **like** to hear to justify the money you're about to spend, but in reality it isn't the most logical approach.

$$NPV = \sum_{t=0}^{n} \frac{CF_t}{(1+r)^t}.$$

The same calculations that work well for larger and sometimes publicly traded companies need to factor in things like a discount rate that in a large part looks at **risk**. If you were valuing an established offline company, you would typically get your 'risk value' (similar to the Beta coefficient in stock analysis) from a similar, publicly traded company. I'm grossly over-simplifying a fairly complicated process, but bear with me - the point remains the same.

Granted, there are now several public internet companies that might exactly match the profile of whatever you're seeking to acquire. However, unless you're in the $10 million + bracket I would argue your 'risk' and their risk is very different.

There is no universally accepted way of valuing a small internet business, so we tend to use a healthy dose of common sense and a combination of looking at comparable transactions and the multiples method.

Let's start at the beginning

To understand where valuations are at now, it's crucial to understand where they began and what sort of went wrong along the way.

When smaller websites started to sell publicly, it happened on Forums in the mid - late 90s with Sitepoint being one of the main proponents. It's important to point out that transactions on the larger side of this segment (*$100K - $2m*) still happened privately, but these were much scarcer then than they are today. Larger sales were often offline businesses with a significant online presence, as opposed to the SaaS or Digital Media companies we know today.

Most, if not all the smaller sites being traded publicly were generic affiliate or AdSense types, so they had very few assets and very few 'moving parts'.

The only thing to separate one site from another was

- **Revenue.** Bear in mind the expenses of one of these sites was usually a few dollars each year on hosting and domain renewal, so this was often very close to profit **and used almost interchangeably**.

- **Traffic.** With a generic AdSense or affiliate site, traffic is proportional to revenue so ultimately if you knew revenue then this factor didn't matter so much.

- **The domain.** Which in the 90s held far less value than it does now.

We can assume that if both the entities being sold (the websites), and the demand for those sites had remained constant, multiples would still be the same today. Inevitably, demand increased and so things proceeded to move on.

Assuming an average domain, and fairly basic methods of tracking and analyzing traffic, it really all came to down to revenue being the deciding factor. This became the de facto way to value a site - as a multiplier of its revenue. Back then I guess, someone, somewhere, decided their selling price should be around **4 - 6 months revenue**.

When consequent sellers looked for a reference as to what they should list their sites for, they would have looked at what similar sites recently sold for on past forum threads, and hence stumbled on the idea of 4 - 6 months revenue. More listings compounded this idea and the **4 - 6x monthly standard** just seemed to stick.

The glory days didn't last for too long.

Value versus Valuations

As an industry, we like to believe we're much more sophisticated today than we used to be.

In the late 90s you had very few options for recruiting new visitors, and even fewer options for monetizing them.

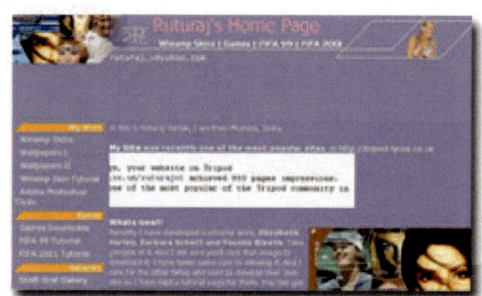

Over time, the typical internet business developed in sophistication and investors began to realize some setups were more favorable than others. There was a widening gap in demand between the more basic sites (*that were prone to almost instant loss of traffic or revenue from over dependence on a few sources*) and a newer breed of more sophisticated sites with multiple channels of income and customer acquisition.

Some websites being sold were now internet businesses, often with the complexities of an offline one. The old 4-6 months revenue valuation model became redundant for them.

These businesses needed a more sophisticated method of valuation. Sites were no longer 'equal', with a clear divide appearing between basic AdSense / Affiliate sites that relied on Google traffic, and the new breed of multi-faceted portals that developed the idea of a customer lifecycle. These newer sites also had varying costs, especially those involved with paid customer acquisition, so now it made sense to **value on net profit** – not gross revenue.

At the same time, an increase in awareness and buyer demand (aka the 'wait, did you just say I can buy a business and get ROI in 6 months?' moment), slowly pushed multiples of even the most mediocre sites up over time.

Throughout all of this, one concept remained the same.

There are three '*tangible intangibles*' that act as primary elements when a buyer thinks about the value of an internet business

1) **Cash Flow** – naturally linked to Profit and Revenue

2) **Traffic** - Customer Acquisition, Traffic Quality and User Engagement

3) **The Domain** - usually nowhere near as important as the previous two, but in some cases a valuable part of the package.

We refer to these as **core elements**, and they're all relatively simple things to assign a dollar value to.

For example, domains are now frequently traded on an open market, so it's easy to get comparable sales to establish an idea of what a premium domain is worth. Likewise, it's often easy to discover a website's RPU (revenue per unique user) or better still, its customer lifetime value, and use this as a measure of how much you could typically earn from each customer / user with a similar demographic profile.

Using these core elements, we can get an idea of a site's value - i.e. its worth to us as a buyer or owner, but here lays the most important concept of this chapter

A site's value is NOT the same as its valuation

A **value** is anchored to the '*tangible intangibles*' like traffic, or cash flow.

A **valuation** is ultimately a made up consensus of what a site is worth based on what people are willing to pay. It often centers on the site's **value**, but there are other factors that come into play

Value is an internal measure, built into the site before a seller makes the decision to sell. This is something rarely affected by the sale process. A Valuation is external; it's a perception of a site's worth and it's affected by external factors like demand, market conditions and current trends. Understanding that concept is the cornerstone of understanding how small web businesses are valued.

We can't necessarily change **value** like traffic or revenue overnight (… *although we have been trying for years*), but it is possible to change a valuation. A seller can easily change a potential buyer's perception with a little work, if they know what factors contribute to it. These factors are referred to as **auxiliary points** and we'll look at these next.

THE NON-THEORY PART YOU'VE POSSIBLY SKIPPED AHEAD TO READ

And if that's the case, **go back** - it's all good reading I promise.

Auxiliary points are factors that contribute to a valuation, besides just the elements of core value. Most of them work to increase a price on the basic laws of economics. If you have more potential buyers you have more demand, and more demand will usually mean a quicker sale at a higher price.

In no particular order they are:

The Core Basics

Does the site have reliable tracking and analytics installed? Is the WHOIS registered to a real company or Mr M Mouse? Are the supplied financials accurate?

All of these things, despite being relatively simple to update and fix affect a valuation. If two identical sites are listed at the same price, and one has Google Analytics whilst the other has a simple stat counter created by the same seller, which do you think is likely to have more competing buyers?

Lists, Social and Members

Having a large and responsive mailing listing or social presence is key to lowering a business's cost of customer acquisition, making it more profitable.
An active social presence also allows for scale and virality – two things we'll explore later on.

The Content

Lots of original and exclusive content such as articles, blog posts, videos or books provide huge value to you as a buyer regardless of whether you use them to attract visitors, sell them on the site or re-purpose them as new materials elsewhere.

Free Cash Flow

Small Internet businesses typically have insanely high net margins. Coupled with substantial revenue, this creates an opportunity to invest the cash elsewhere, or further develop the site you've purchased.

Critical Mass

Platform driven businesses such as marketplaces, forums or dating sites, need to achieve critical mass in order to thrive. Those businesses that have (i.e. they've solved the chicken and egg problem to get enough of one side to attract the other) will be worth significantly more than those that haven't.

Traffic Diversification

Over dependence on one source of traffic creates a business that can easily see its new customers disappear overnight. A website that has multiple streams of traffic from social, referrals, paid acquisition and search is a more stable business with a higher valuation.

Revenue Diversification

Like traffic, depending on just one stream of revenue is a risk but it's also leaving money on the table. A website that can monetize the same visitor at various times through different channels will usually be more profitable than one that can't.

Documented Systems and Maintenance Requirements

Whilst no business ever 'runs on autopilot', some businesses take more resources to operate than others. When we look at maintenance from a buyer perspective, we often look at all the tasks that need to be performed on a regular basis that haven't been accounted for on a profit and loss statement – in other words, someone (usually the owner) is doing it for free and if you acquire the site, that will be you.

Trust and Transparency

Interestingly, trust and transparency goes a long way towards determining a site's final selling price. People are more likely to trust sellers that have a legitimate online presence and can provide some recourse if things go wrong.

Imagine a site being sold by a public figure, active in online communities and therefore with something to lose if a deal went sour. Compare that to another being sold by an elusive owner based in another continent, most buyers would pay more for the security offered by the former.

Sales Partners and Affiliates

A site that has recruited hundreds of established affiliates to sell its products doesn't just have traffic diversification, but it also has a system that allows for rapid scale. By themselves, strategic partnerships and affiliate relationships have little to no value, but when they're part of a greater system (the business), the value is apparent in the higher prices these businesses attract.

Reputation and Brand

Business owners often confuse having a brand with having a logo and a color scheme.

Smaller Internet businesses rarely achieve brand status, but it's not uncommon (especially with software or authority blogs) to see sites for sale that have completely dominated their niche and acquire a significant amount of traffic through word of mouth or referrals on the strength of their product offering.

The Niche

Having a presence in some niches / verticals will always be more valuable than being in others. This is partly due to the size of the market, and the amount advertisers are prepared to spend.

If you had two identically performing businesses, but one was in Finance and the other was in Beauty, the former would have a higher valuation. Any smart buyer would know that they can probably earn far more from one finance customer than they could from a beauty one.

Also, knowing the niche has growth potential and is also large enough to make a substantial profit is an important factor too.

IP, Software and Products

A business that has intellectual property rights, or includes custom software or products with the sale, gives a buyer some barriers to entry against new competition.

All of these factors contribute to a site's valuation, but it's rarely a conscious process.

There is no quantitative way to measure critical mass; a site either has it or doesn't. Likewise, there's no sensible way to measure the value of bespoke products or IP that may be included with the sale.

Factoring in everything above is more of a subconscious process that you'll to go through to consider an asset's worth to you personally. We covered this briefly earlier when we looked at setting your personal criteria for knowing what types of sites to buy.

Even if every point on the list above is something new, you'll quickly learn (through absorption) to qualify potential purchases using those points as a backbone. The more acquisitions you study, and the more you question why they are, or possibly aren't good purchases, the more it will become second nature.

DECIDING HOW MUCH TO PAY

You don't necessarily need to understand the theory to do a basic website valuation, but having that knowledge will make everything seem more logical in practice.

The two simplest methods to establish a sensible price for a site are

1) Pay a specialist to conduct a valuation **or**

2) Use recent comparable listings and transactions to get an idea of what similar businesses sold for and use this as a starting point.

Each year we publish the **Website Buyer's Report** (centurica.com/website-buyers-report). You'll find all the key figures you need, like valuation multiples and median asking prices for a variety of established internet businesses sold during the previous year.

This is a good start, but I'd also encourage you to look at active listings to find something closely related to the site you're trying to value in terms of size, niche and business model to get an even better idea of a sensible price. You'll find a comparable multiple that you can use as a benchmark.

At the time of writing this book, that multiple will typically be between **1.8x** and **4x annual net profits**. So for example, a business generating $100,000 each year in net profit will sell for between $180,000 and $400,000.

The problem with multiples

The above approach is relatively sensible, and will give you a crude valuation on any internet business.

The problem is that as a method, it's flawed. It can cause you to miss out on better deals, because relying on a multiple alone doesn't paint the full picture. That's where the auxiliary points we covered earlier come into play. I'll try to put it all into context.

Before deciding Internet business and buying websites was the route I wanted to take, I had a relatively successful offline service business.

About three years into being established and probably a year before committing fully to web, there was also a short foray into retail. The kind of foray I really don't like to talk about.

The kind of foray that didn't end well.

If you've ever owned a retail business then you'll probably know how difficult it can be just to turn a profit, especially at the start of the financial crisis. Rarely do you find entrepreneurs who master retail, but also own service or web based companies too. It has an all-or-nothing nature about it.

Failing massively will teach you a lot of things, but my expensive retail education provided a lesson that ported well into the online acquisitions that I do today. One of the golden rules of retail is to always pay for premium space in a grade A location. In hindsight, everything about that makes sense.

Take the UK as an example.

In comparison to the US, we have less emphasis on Malls, and stores are usually clustered into central shopping areas or 'high streets'. A 1,000 square foot space in a grade B – C location several miles outside of the city would cost around **£18,000 (approx $30,000) to rent each year**.

The same size space in a Grade A Location (e.g. Manchester / Leeds City Centre) will cost anything from **£36,000 to £150,000 per year** depending on which part of the city it is in.

As a rookie retailer, my choice was to start with the grade B space and accept there would be fewer customers but at a lower level of risk. At the time, I failed to realize that Grade A space would not only mean more footfall, but also

- **Less seasonality**, as visitors are likely to be there all year round.

- An **increase in revenue**. This meant other fixed costs that remained constant regardless of the location like products costs, utilities or staff, would be a much smaller percentage of turnover. In turn, the business was less likely to be affected by inevitable fluctuations in those same costs.

- The **synergy of more recommendations** via word of mouth and more advertising / exposure from people seeing your store.

From an Internet Business perspective, the same applies to buying the largest business you can afford, but even more importantly, knowing when it's ok to venture outside the safety of set multiples.

As a buyer, I've often become too caught up with the 'multiple' a business is selling for, and totally forgotten to question the value the business holds both now, and the potential value several years down the line.

There are four typical scenarios where paying above your average multiple can be a good idea.

1) Your strategy is to hold onto an asset for value appreciation and / or operational profit.

Four years ago, I spoke to a buyer who would pay 1.8x annual net profit for any good, safe web business that came his way. At the time, 1.8x net was a very fair price to pay, so he managed to amass a significant amount of inventory in a short space of time.

Other buyers thought he was crazy, often over paying where he didn't have to. Many average sites at the time sold for 1.4x – 1.7x. His strategy allowed him first refusal on deals that sell for 2.5x – 3x today, because of their strength as an asset and the increase in overall market prices.

When the average valuation was 4x monthly net (back when the Internet was in black and white), people baulked at paying 1x annual net. The same goes for property, shares or anything else that is steadily appreciating in value – what might seem like overpaying now, not only allows you access to and first refusal on the best purchases, but it later turns out to be a wise decision if those assets appreciate in value.

As long as demand outstrips supply, prices should continue to rise for good assets, as they will always be the ones in demand. If you plan to hold onto the site for at least one year, then the capital appreciation alone can often 'correct' the higher multiple you've paid to purchase it.

2) When an asset has a substantially positive growth curve

Interestingly, when many people look at an asset, they look for a sales decline as part of their due diligence, but rarely look for a positive growth curve.

When we see insane valuations of SaaS businesses being sold or acqui-hired, those valuations are often (but not always) backed up by two things:

- **Consistent and viral user growth**. Businesses like WhatsApp aren't just acquiring huge numbers of users, but the rate of acquisition is rapidly increasing too, meaning where the company is this month is likely to be dwarfed by where it will be in a year.

- **Recurring revenues with good retention**. Knowing that customers who have already been acquired will contribute $X over time, makes it easier to justify paying 4x – 8x annual net, versus a business that's currently earning the same amount but is more likely to lose revenue if new client acquisition slows down.

Ideally, the best acquisitions we can make will have both of those qualities 'built-in', meaning any improvements you make or new clients you acquire will only add to existing growth rather than maintain it. In this case, paying 'Silicon Valley' money can sometimes be justified.

3) Highly Passive Opportunities
It's amazing how many people still think

- Totally passive income on the web exists

- Content / AdSense Sites offer the most passive form of internet business

No business will ever be totally passive – it's a sliding scale with certain low maintenance opportunities on one side and all-in high maintenance ones on the other.

Those low maintenance or highly passive opportunities can naturally command a higher multiple, simply because you're able to achieve the same return with less work.

4) The acquisition is just plain strategic

A strategic acquisition is one that has more value to the acquirer than to the average potential buyer.

For example, if you own a network of pet related sites, acquiring a DIY kennel building product would be a smart idea. Your cost of customer acquisition will be minimal compared to someone starting from scratch. Not only do you make more profit from the added traffic you can send over at a lower cost, but some of that site's list may be potential customers for your other sites too.

Let's assume the hypothetical DIY product site spends $100K annually on paid traffic. Over a year, the site earns $50K in net profit. You could halve the amount being spent on paid traffic and send visitors from your existing pet properties instead. The money you save ($50K) would go directly into profit giving you an annual net of $50K + $50K = $100K for the DIY product site.

Now, a valuation that's 4 or 5x at a net of $50K, becomes 2x – 2.5x at a net of $100K.

Buying a Website with the full picture

Multiples will always be a simple and quick method of assessing how an investment stacks up in comparison to other investments you can make with the same capital, but they shouldn't be the final decision.

Knowing how much to pay for a business should ultimately align with your personal goals for that investment, but never prevent or limit you from purchasing something strong.

If you ever have any doubts, speak to anyone who has owned a home in a good area for more than 15 years and ask them if they considered the purchase to be expensive when they bought it. Investors with a long term view will always be rewarded, provided they make a stable and smart purchase, backed by good research and better due diligence.

07.
PORTFOLIO STARS

73	GOLDEN RETENTION
80	TRUE VIRALITY
84	ABOVE AVERAGE CUSTOMER LIFETIME VALUES
88	PROFITABLE PAID USER ACQUISITION
92	STRATEGIC ACQUISITIONS
97	SUSTAINABLE MONTH ON MONTH GROWTH

PORTFOLIO STARS

Not all acquisitions are created equal.

For anyone just starting, their goal is often just not to lose any money. Each time you sell and trade up, you become a little better at knowing what works for you and how to extract maximum value. Even if you only ever purchase one site and hold onto it indefinitely, the lessons you learn along the way are invaluable.

With enough time or trades under your belt, you start to learn which types of purchases are your ideal scenarios. The types of businesses that you will pay over the odds for without a second thought, because their ownership gives more certainty of financial success. These types of sites are what I call **Portfolio Stars**, and in my opinion, the types of purchases you should always be on the look-out for.

These are acquisitions with positive metrics that make the deal almost too good to refuse. Even if the multiple is comparatively higher than other deals you might also be considering, these types of businesses will always sell quickly.

As the majority of sellers do such a terrible job of financial and performance reporting in their business, these positive metrics can often go undiscovered, which means you'll have to do some work in calculating them.

This is the extra 10% that most buyers either fail to understand, or fail to use because it's too much effort. Looking at acquisitions based on the following metrics will **always** give you the upper hand over buyers who only consider profit and traffic when assessing the value of a potential purchase.

It's worth noting the following types of deals are incredibly difficult to find in the sub $500K price range, but they do exist. Finding one at the right price will usually justify the time spent searching for it.

GOLDEN RETENTION

Retention, in any recurring revenue or membership business, refers to the average duration of time a paying customer remains active. It's such an important metric for certain types of business, yet it's surprising how many owners have no idea what their retention numbers are.

Occasionally, you'll find a business where the retention is strong enough to guarantee payback even with no further user acquisition. In other words, any users that you do acquire are guaranteed to be additional profit and not required to maintain or support the business.

This is one of those rare gems where it's almost always worth paying significantly over the average multiple when you discover it. Naturally, this relies on the business having a recurring revenue model and is most common with businesses that either:

- **Have a high product value and a high cost of switching.** For example, Hosting, Data Management, Infrastructure / Platforms as a Service and SaaS Apps aimed at an enterprise market.

- **Have a very low monthly cost and a wide existing user base.** For example, newsletter subscriptions, graphic & template sites or subscription commerce businesses with a low value product (e.g. snack boxes, or pet products).

Here are some numbers from a real example I found four months ago prior to writing this (*I'm looking at deals daily and have only one example to share – that should show you how rare this is*).

The business was a **PaaS** (Platform as a Service) website that sold infrastructure and cloud hosting to developers who wanted to use a specific database technology popular with large web applications (*NoSQL*). This is a smaller acquisition than you'll typically find, especially for hosting businesses, but one that illustrates the point well.

NOSQL DATABASE HOST

```
Supplying   hosting   and   infrastructure   for
developers  who  need  to  host  their  database
remotely, for speed and redundancy.


Annual Revenue: $18,000  |  Annual Net: $15,000

Asking Price: $25,000    |  Multiple: 1.67x
```

At the time of sale, the company had just 55 users. In my opinion the owners had given up far too quickly and were selling at a ridiculously low price. They were selling because growth was not enough to make quitting their current jobs (*as overpaid developers in the valley*) worthwhile.

Annual gross revenue was around **$18K** and net profit **$15K**. The owners wanted $25K for the business and I advised the buyer to offer **$30K**, as there were already several interested parties on the verge of closing the deal.

This was a classic example of entrepreneurs failing to see the value in their business because they didn't understand the numbers. Their official reason for selling was that they were working on a bigger project in their day jobs and didn't have time to commit to this business. Interestingly though, there were very little maintenance requirements outside of setting up new users on Amazon's Infrastructure which I believe provided the backbone for their service. Most of that setup was automated.

I spoke to the sellers directly to get a better understanding about the business. The real reason for wanting to sell stemmed from becoming disheartened that they had a **high churn rate** (customers who stopped using the service).

After putting in hard work blogging and writing how-to guides to recruit new users, they had simultaneously lost some existing customers too and felt it was a zero sum game. A few months prior, they had also attempted paid advertising and failed. I assume this was due to their inexperience, but with failure in different areas mounting, they had simply given up. *The luxury of a $150K salary with perks kind of helps you to do that.*

Considering they currently had the most active users that they've ever had (55), now seemed like a good time to pursue a quick sale. What they possibly failed to realize was that even with no new customers, a new owner would still generate more than **$38K** from recurring monthly payments, by the time the last customer was likely to leave. In other words, there was a very high probability that even in worst case scenario - no new users, a new owner would recoup their entire investment making this a worthy gamble to take.

In our research, we performed a real quick and dirty retention analysis. You can see how it was created on the next page.

It's worth mentioning that not all of this estimated $38K would be profit, but they had very little cost in the business. Their provider, Amazon, only billed them for what they used. They didn't have the monthly overhead of renting their own servers and had very few support tickets. Most of their revenue ended up as net profit.

The new owner who acquired this business has being operating for around three months at time of writing.

In the last month alone, he's managed to increase new sign-ups through paid placements and reviews on blogs. He also made a smart gamble to increase the minimum billing period to **3 months** rather than 1 month.

Ironically, increasing the minimum billing period which took a few minutes to implement, dwarfed what was achieved through arranging paid placements and reviews. This helps prove the point from the first chapter; it's better to understand **internet business** before understanding **internet marketing**.

CALCULATING AVERAGE RETENTION - A QUICK PRIMER

The owner of the business we just looked believed they had a high churn (*i.e. low retention*), but in reality, their expectations were just unrealistic.

To test this theory, we had to calculate the **retention period** first.

You can use several formulas to calculate a site's retention, but this one is possibly the easiest and most practical bearing in mind the information you can get access to. It involves some manual data crunching but it's something you can easily **outsource** if there are a lot of transactions.

> The seller supplied two lists. One of **all customer transactions**, including those customers who had lapsed (*no longer a paying user*) and another of transactions from currently **active customers only**. Naturally, they were concerned with privacy, so they replaced any personal details like the customer name or email address, with an identifier - so customer 123, customer 234 etc.

Transaction Date	Transaction Amount ($)	Customer Identifier
2013-09-03	$46.00	1241
2013-09-03	$18.00	768
2013-09-04	$72.00	113

> Most sellers will be happy to oblige if they're genuine and they believe you are too. It's a simple export from their shopping cart software or merchant account and no sensitive data is at risk once they replace those details. At this point, you're taking the information supplied on face value. Once you've begun **full due diligence**, validating the details in this export with real customer data will be your priority.

Using Excel (*the only Microsoft product still worth owning?*), take the date a customer first appeared. Add one month to this date, as every customer signed up for a minimum of one month, so even if they only made one billing cycle, they were technically still a customer for 1 month. Take the date a customer last appeared or cancelled the service too. This is used to create a table that shows the duration each person was a customer for and then an average duration for the entire list. **The average in our example was 16 months**.

Take the sheet of **active customers only** and note the date that each active user became a client alongside their identifier. In the next column, add **16 months** (our average) to that date to get an idea of when they would statistically stop being an active user.

By taking a total of users each month from this spreadsheet, build a table that looks at the number of active users each month for the next 17 months from owning the business if no further users joined. Based on the average we calculated, 17 months would technically be the point where no more users would be left if no more joined post purchase.

Month after Acquisition	1	2	3	4	5	6
Number of Customers	55	53	51	49	48	48
Total Revenue ($)	3,740	3,604	3,468	3,332	3,264	3,264
Cumulative Revenue ($)	3,740	7,344	10,812	14,144	17,408	20,672

Month after Acquisition	7	8	9	10	11	12
Number of Customers	46	41	38	35	32	24
Total Revenue ($)	3,128	2,788	2,584	2,380	2,176	1,632
Cumulative Revenue ($)	23,800	26,588	29,172	31,552	33,728	35,360

Month after Acquisition	13	14	15	16	17
Number of Customers	18	13	7	4	0
Total Revenue ($)	1,224	884	476	272	0
Cumulative Revenue ($)	36,854	37,468	37,944	38,216	0

When it's not that straightforward

Working with real data, nothing is ever linear.

You'll always experience some deviation from what you expect to be the end result. In the earlier example, our linear assumption is that every customer will be an active user for exactly 16 months based on the average.

You can never account for the unknown.

Remove some uncertainty by calculating your averages or assumptions from a large enough pool of data.

There are some situations that can unexpectedly throw your results off and it's useful to know what they are.

Cohorts

In the case of recurring revenue web businesses, a cohort is usually a set of users that joined during a particular event or time frame.

This is important, because those users can behave differently to others. Using our earlier example, the company may have had some sign-ups come from a promotion they did with a tech deal site like **App Sumo** for example.

Assuming the deal was a discount for X months, these sign-ups might behave differently to normal sign-ups. They are more likely to cancel when the deal is over, making the retention rate for this specific cohort of users much shorter. Likewise, a company will usually get better as time goes on, so an average spend for an ecommerce site's customers who used the site in year one, might be lower than those who used it in year two.

Cohorts give you more accuracy in predicting customer behavior, but they can over-complicate the otherwise simple task of guiding you to a 'should I invest or not' decision. Remember to take a big picture view first to decide if splitting the data into cohorts is really necessary.

Competition

Increased competition or new entrants to your niche will always affect what your current customers do. The exception is where they're locked in by a contract or binding agreement. Remember to look at the potential threat of new entrants.

Enterprise software or PaaS (Platform as a Service) has never been a 'fashionable industry'.

In the case of our example earlier, new competition wouldn't be too much of a concern. The flipside would be a site that is a social app or subscription commerce site for example, where well-funded new entrants appear almost daily.

Technology

Changes in technology can mean you're unable to offer now the same service you will offer several years in the future. The best examples are businesses that rely on third party sites or APIs (*e.g. scrapping Google results or using the Twitter API*), but don't have a paid arrangement in place.

API terms and conditions frequently change, and it's not uncommon for people who have built large applications to find themselves with a redundant tool when it changes.

You should be trying to avoid acquisitions with unreliable third party dependence as part of your due diligence. If you do proceed, and you are making speculative calculations, remember to factor this in.

TRUE VIRALITY

A simple way of describing the Virality or **Viral Coefficient** of a business is simply the number of additional users or customers that are recruited as a direct result of existing customer activity.

This comes in various forms in the types of businesses you'll see for sale:

- **Ecommerce Businesses** that allow customers to share or brag about their purchase through Facebook or Pinterest. This is effectively advertising to every user's social network for free.

- **Games and Mobile Apps** with an invite function that encourages users to recruit friends to join.

- **SaaS applications** that implement social sharing to view what a user has created or curated, but require the person viewing to create an account of their own.

You can calculate a website's **Viral Coefficient** as

Average Number of Shares (*or Invites or Emails*) sent by one customer

The Percentage that convert to customers

For example, if you purchased an ecommerce store where 50 customers shared their purchase a total of 30 times, and that resulted in 5 sales, your viral coefficient would be

$$(30/50) * (5/30) = \mathbf{0.1}$$

A viral coefficient of less than 1 indicates no viral growth – in other words, you would need to recruit clients using paid advertising or organic acquisition in order to continue growing the business.

On the flip-side, imagine a SaaS Application that allows entrepreneurs to network and connect with other similar companies online. Every user that joins connects to their LinkedIn account and sends out **10** invites. From those invites an average of **2** new users sign up.

This business has a viral coefficient of

$$(10/1) * (2/10) = \mathbf{2}$$

A number above 1 indicates **virality**. This is exponential growth without any acquisition efforts on behalf of the owner.

A business that grows without any owner involvement is a rare find. It's almost like someone gift-wrapped your success and handed it over with a bow on. It's highly unlikely that you'll find a truly viral business for sale that's both **obviously** viral and profitable.

Knowing a business is viral is usually enough to prevent most people wanting to sell. However, having insights into the seller's business that maybe the seller doesn't have themselves can often help you acquire valuable businesses at a fraction of their true cost.

The following scenarios are fairly common, but often lead to a situation where virality is present, but hasn't yet been exploited or in some cases, recognized.

A long viral cycle time

Some internet businesses have an amazing viral coefficient, but fail to realize it due to a long viral cycle time.

This is the duration of time in-between a user signing up, and another individual who they referred becoming a user themselves.

For some sites this is really short. For example, you read an article on **Buzzfeed** and share it. Someone in your friend's feed on **Facebook** reads what you've shared and does the same themselves. In this case, the viral cycle time is less than 1 day but for other sites it can be months.

A site that allows users to share short videos they've edited (*like **Vine***) could recruit a user but fail to see referrals from that new user until they've created and uploaded videos themselves. In some cases, this could be weeks if not months.

The best viral acquisition opportunities are usually found in relatively new sites (1 – 2 years old) that are yet to hit critical mass. Often, the seller has given up prematurely, not realizing they have virality but it just takes a long time to 'cycle'.

Poor monetization

Virality is useless without good monetization or Silicon Valley investors. You can use this to your advantage.

I've seen businesses for sale that have experienced viral growth (secure file storage, mobile games and MMORPGs), but failed to monetize their users adequately. Each new user comes on-board at a loss, due to the additional server and bandwidth requirements needed to support them.

If you have a clear path to making a profit from this user through developing the businesses monetization strategy, you can acquire the site significantly below cost and almost instantly increase its value through a few well-placed changes.

Hybrid virality

Some businesses are not technically viral, but may well be close with a viral coefficient (VC) of 0.7 – 0.99.

In this case, it's not a total write off as far as acquiring a site with virality is concerned. Every step closer to a VC of 1, means a lower cost of overall customer acquisition even if you do have to supplement it with paid marketing.

For example, if you're looking at a social app with a VC of 0.8, and one with a VC of 0, you know that you'll have to spend less with the first site than you would with the second to acquire the same amount of customers. Some of those customers in the site with a 0.8 VC would be 'free' or acquired as a result of viral activity.

The majority of sites for sale have no viral element at all (i.e. a VC of 0).

It stands to reason that acquiring a site with even the slightest element of virality in a niche where your competition doesn't have this, means you can pay less to acquire the same number of visitors and gain the upper hand.

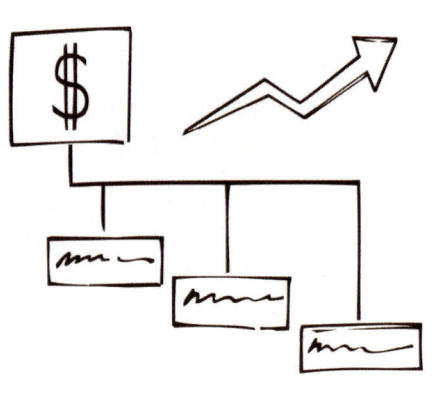

ABOVE AVERAGE CUSTOMER LIFETIME VALUES

Customer Lifetime Value or **CLTV** is the amount of gross profit (or in some cases gross revenue) you can extract from a customer during their lifespan with you.

There are several ways to calculate a business's CLTV. Again, it's another useful metric that sellers rarely know. In keeping with the theme of speed over accuracy, here are the two I would prefer to use.

i) The Quicker, less accurate method

You calculate the average retention period as shown earlier, and the average monthly or daily spend by looking at the **total spend for a customer** divided by the **duration of time** they have been one. The CLTV is simply the **average retention period** multiplied by the **average spend**. From our example earlier (the PaaS provider) it was

$$\$68 \ (average \ monthly \ spend) * 16 \ (16 \ months \ average \ retention \ period)$$
$$=$$
$$\$1,088$$

ii) The (slightly) more accurate method if you don't have the retention period

You take the **total spend per unique user** for anyone who has been a customer for longer than say 3 months.

Next, take an average across all users and use this as your figure for CLTV. This approach makes working with segments easier, as you can calculate the CLTV for different sets of users and apply a weighting to each for more accuracy.

For example, if 20% of a site's users are Enterprise users with an average CLTV of $1,000, whilst 80% are small businesses with a CLTV of $500, a more accurate way of calculating your CLTV would be to use a weighted average:

$$(\$1{,}000 * 0.2) + (\$500 * 0.8) = \mathbf{\$600}$$

If we were to use a normal average for the scenario above, our CLTV figure would be **$750**, an amount that doesn't take into account enterprise users being in the minority. This could potentially lead you to over pay for the business.

The beauty of a well-developed funnel

At the start of this book, we looked at how a well-developed customer funnel is responsible for delivering higher customer lifetime values. Developing a profitable funnel along with a series of upsells, downsells and related products, is as much art as it is science.

Some operators have mastered building profitable funnels in their niche because they understand the customer well, and test frequently. Many of the previous examples of 'magic numbers' focus on businesses with a recurring revenue model. Funnels are something that you can get in almost every type of potential website acquisition, making this a common benefit to find.

The advantages of being able to extract more from a customer are leverage and customer acquisition. More leverage in that each customer will earn you far more than it will in a comparative business and better customer acquisition in that you can afford to pay more to acquire a user. This makes it incredibly difficult for new or even established competitors to beat the price you're prepared to pay without making a loss. This results in more options and better placements. This is an advantage that's almost always worth paying more for.

Consider this example

Two businesses both compete in the field of **property investment info products** and share similar revenues and profit. **Site A** is being sold at a significantly lower multiple than **Site B** – **2.3x** and **3.1x** respectively.

Site A generates most of its income from front-end sales and has a **CLTV of $150**.

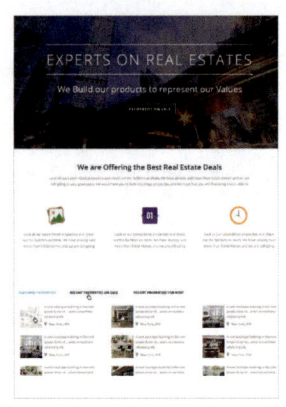

SITE A – PROPERTY INVESTMENT COURSE

A series of videos covering the basics of investing in property.

Annual Revenue: $230,000 | **Annual Net:** $187,000

Asking Price: $430,000 | **Multiple:** 2.3x

Users are taken to a landing page that offers a video course on property investing for $100. They have a few limited upsells (additional videos) on that sales page. Once a user makes a purchase, they are never contacted again.

Site B generates its income from a wide variety of products and services. It has half the number of customers as Site A but has a **CLTV of $300**. Users are initially taken to an opt-in page for a free mini course on property investing. Once they sign up, they're sent an invitation to a webinar. On this webinar, they are sold the same $100 course offered by Site A. Those who purchased the $100 product are also offered membership to an 'VIP' course that pays affiliate commissions of anything up to $1,000.

SITE B – PROPERTY INVESTMENT COURSE

A series of educational resources covering the basics of property investment.

Annual Revenue: $230,000 | **Annual Net:** $187,000

Asking Price: $580,000 | **Multiple:** 3.1x

Those who didn't attend the webinar or didn't purchase are offered a lower value product at $49, a week or so later. If they fail to purchase the $49 product, their details are sold as a lead to a coaching floor (call center), who then try to sell personal development products one to one by phone. (*Sure, it's a cheap shot, but this is a fictional example and we're not here to judge!*)

Site B does far more with less. You can be sure that every $1 or hour you spend on marketing would be put to infinitely better use than with Site A that has the same revenues but less overall potential as is.

You also have the option of paying more than Site A to recruit a new user. Up to $299.99 would technically make you a profit. This is a figure that would bankrupt Site A which only makes $150 per user.

As the owner of Site B

- You can use aggressive tactics to ensure only you have access to the best direct advertising placements by buying 'run of site'

- You can offer a far bigger payout to affiliates who would then most likely choose to promote you over your competitor.

- You can afford to always rank high in paid search and paid social as you're prepared to make the platform more money than your competitor by spending more for each click.

On the flip side, there's still an opportunity in buying Site A and duplicating the funnel of Site B to drastically improve the business. That naturally depends on whether you're going for an **operational** or **development** play, but this is the danger and the opportunity that many new buyers confuse.

On the surface, it might seem that Site B is easy to replicate, especially if you sign up to all their marketing and go through the funnel yourself. In reality, most good sites are far more complex than they appear to the end user. The money spent to acquire one, is a short cut to not having to endure the learning curve yourself.

PROFITABLE PAID USER ACQUISITION

The majority of internet businesses that you'll find for sale rely on organic search traffic as their primary way to deliver new visitors.

To the rookie buyer, this is a huge positive. Search traffic is usually highly targeted, converts well and best of all it's free. If you're currently scratching your head thinking "what could go wrong?" read on. This section is for you.

Remember Panda and Penguin?

If you've ever woken up and checked your stats to find a business you own has lost more than half of its traffic, it's highly unlikely you'll ever forget that day. This is what happens continually to millions of site owners whenever a new search update is released. They find themselves in the loser's corner instead of celebrating with the winners. If that site happened to be one you purchased just months ago, the blow will be even more severe.

The unpredictable nature of Google and Bing makes them a poor source of customer acquisition, and a threat to your business if you rely on it. However, it's not just about the instability.

Sites that rely on search traffic are notoriously difficult to scale. Everyone knows some SEO just like everyone in the 80s thought they knew a little Kung Fu, but improving rankings is notoriously difficult in most industries. The exceptions are keywords or niches where there is little traffic or competition.

However, making a 20% improvement on a 200 searches per month keyword is never going to build an empire.

This is why sites with profitable paid acquisition campaigns are worth more than their weight in bitcoin. Traffic that you've paid for is reliable, scalable, easy to split test with and most importantly, something you as the owner control. As long as there's a financial relationship in place, there's little need to worry about that traffic source drying up one day, or that link being replaced or getting lost as people inevitably stop sharing it. You will always receive traffic as long as you're prepared to pay.

This makes websites that already have a profitable paid campaign in place valuable, as the owner has already answered the questions of:

- Will paid traffic convert at a good enough rate to make a profit
- Are my profit margins high enough to support paid traffic and
- What tweaks or changes do I need to make on the site and in my campaigns to make this campaign profitable.

Setting up profitable paid campaigns isn't just time consuming – it's expensive. You can waste anything upwards of $10K in a few days, testing sources that don't convert well enough. There's huge value in having this already done for you.

How to spot a profitable paid campaign

Theoretically, you should be able to look for an acquisition where the owner has declared regular advertising spend, but as always, it's not that simple.

From my experience, many (> 30%) of the sites that are running paid traffic campaigns are not doing so profitably. It's the old "my Advertising works, I just don't know which half" story. Owners will see a profit overall, but not really know how much of that can be attributed to the traffic they've purchased.

This becomes more difficult with sites that have a long lead-time to a customer purchase; the user might discover the site through an advert on a social platform for example, but return 30 or so days later from an email they were sent after they signed up and made a purchase.

Without the site's analytics setup to track this correctly, that purchase will be attributed to email. If they're not using tracking links correctly it may even show as 'Direct'. It could appear that their paid campaign which initially sent that visitor is nowhere near as profitable as it actually is.

Even with something like Google Analytics set up and properly tracking conversions, you still have the issue of attribution. If a visitor sees an Advert on Google and visits your site, but then returns and buys after seeing a retargeted advert on Facebook, which one do you attribute the sale to? Google Analytics have made this easier with Multi Channel conversion reporting, but it's far from being straightforward.

There's no way of avoiding a situation like this short of 'fixing' their analytics and waiting to see what happens. Realistically, that's out of your remit whilst you're just assessing the purchase. The good news though is that it's unlikely that a conversion will be attributed to a paid campaign when that's not the case.

Assuming their tracking and analytics is setup legitimately, if they are showing 20 sales for example from paid traffic for that month, it's usually going to be slightly more in reality. This means a campaign that appears profitable by even $1 in the seller's analytics, is usually more profitable than it looks and so there's the opportunity to scale it.

What to do when there's no conversion tracking

Sometimes, the seller won't be tracking paid conversions at all. I've no idea why someone wouldn't when they're paying for traffic, but it's worryingly common. There's still the option of a crude educated guess with their cooperation. You can also do this with the information in the sale brochure or listing, so it's something you can do ahead of time to qualify potential stars.

First, you'll need the site's gross profit per user i.e. the total gross profit for that month divided the number of unique visits for the same period.

From their paid traffic account (e.g. Adwords or Facebook Ads), get the average cost per visitor across the entire campaign. If you don't have access to this information, you can make an educated guess at the keywords that are most likely to convert, and find typical costs per click from Google or Facebook's Ad planning tools.

Is this figure at least 20% below the site's gross profit per user?

If so, this is usually an indication that a paid campaign could be profitable, but it is still an educated guess at best. The conversion from paid traffic is rarely the same as the conversion on the site overall that will include organic and social traffic. 1,000 paid visits may not generate the same amount of revenue as 1,000 organic ones so use this method with caution.

This approach isn't accurate, but it will give you enough of a start to decide whether it's worth requesting further information to make a more informed decision.

Paused campaigns and bullshit

You'll frequently see situations where an owner has made an entry for advertising on their monthly profit and loss statement some months earlier, but that expense no longer exists. Assuming they're not hiding the cost to make the business appear more profitable (*oh …. it happens*), the most frequent reasons we've heard are

- *"We were getting to many orders so had to stop the campaign to deal with the overflow"*

- *"It was costing too much and affecting our cash flow"*

- *"We only turn it on in quiet times when we need a boost."*

In my experience, an owner with a business that they want to grow will never pause or stop a profitable campaign. Doing so usually indicates either it wasn't profitable or they had no way of tracking whether or not it was.

If a seller couldn't get paid advertising to work, it doesn't necessarily mean you can't.

Many people have a poor understanding of how paid advertising works, especially on Google's ad network. You have to use your discretion as to whether this would be something worth pursuing if you took over and whether you could see success where the previous owner had failed.

STRATEGIC ACQUISITIONS

Every business essentially has two kinds of buyer – multiple driven and strategic.

Multiple driven buyers care about making an investment that will perform as well as or at least relative to other investments they can make at a similar level.

This often means paying no more than an accepted, average multiple.

They can do this because there is no strategic or logical reason to favor one particular investment over another. If one site allows payback in 2 years and another does payback in 4, the shorter payback will always win (although **we** know that's not always the case).

Strategic buyers look at the situation differently and have some 'emotional buy-in'. When I say emotional, it's emotional in the sense that this specific site matters more than any other generic investment. These are people who possibly own similar properties and have a very clear plan for what to do once they own a new site to extract maximum value.

It could be cross selling products, services or signups to other properties in their portfolio, or it could be filling the top of their user acquisition funnel on another site with leads. We can break strategic acquisitions down by the buyer's motivation.

Traffic Acquisitions

Consider this example:

A site that receives **10,000 visitors per month** generates **$400** monthly via Google AdSense assuming a **$0.04 RPU** (typical of an AdSense site that you would find at auction). This is **Site A**, and the seller asks for **$19,000**. At a multiple of approximately **4x annual net**, this is likely be out of your price range if you're a multiple-driven buyer.

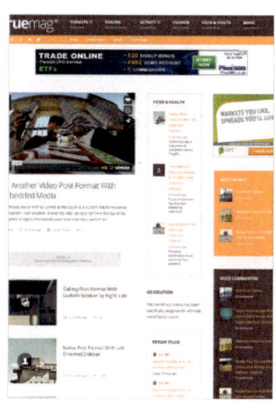

SITE A - CONTENT SITE

Basic Adsense site offering help on improving your resume and dressing for an interview.

Annual Revenue: $4,800 | **Annual Net:** $4,750

Asking Price: $19,000 | **Multiple:** 4x

Now imagine you currently pay **$2 per click** through Google Adwords for a different site that you already own - **Site B**. This is in the same niche of jobs and recruitment, and has the same customer profile as Site A.

Imagine you purchase Site A, and feature a prominent banner across the leaderboard that drives visitors to your existing site (B) with a great offer. You also email every new signup to site A with a link to this site too.

If **15%** of the visits to Site A, converted to visitors to Site B, that would equal **1,500 visits per month**. This is the same amount of visits that **$3,000** would buy you if you were to do it through advertising.

At **$19,000**, the site will effectively pay for itself in just **6 months** making every month thereafter profit. That's also totally ignoring the added benefit of any mailing lists the site may have, social media presences, products, additional positions in the SERPs for valuable keywords (*that now can't be occupied by a competitor*) and naturally, the revenue it generates from the ad positions you haven't used.

Now, 4x net makes sense.

This is just one way that you would make a strategic acquisition. It's fairly common as so many websites for sale at the lower end of the market are relatively under-monetized.

Synergy or portfolio acquisitions

Sometimes an acquisition will make sense because of similar assets that you already own.

A portfolio of assets in a similar vertical, will usually sell for more than the sum of the individual sites. If your portfolio value exceeds $2 million, you also have the option of selling to the various boutique private equity firms that have begun to appear. They tend to specialize in digital assets valued between $2 million and $10 million.

There are also huge benefits while you own the portfolio too.

Firstly, there's the idea of **vertical integration** - owning various parts of the 'production' path. A good example might be if you owned a blog that taught new entrepreneurs how to make money online and generated revenue from affiliate product sales. If you acquired a Clickbank affiliate site aimed at this same market, you would become one of your own main advertisers and own this part of your customer's journey.

You could take it one step further and purchase a recurring revenue Member Site that helped those entrepreneurs on their journey to profitability, creating more synergy along the way. Rather than pay three times to acquire each visitor to each business you now own, you would only pay once. You could drive them to your other properties for almost no additional spend.

On the flip side, you also have **horizontal integration**. If you acquire three ecommerce companies then you can significantly reduce your cost of customer support, warehousing and marketing through centralization.

Likewise if you have several content sites, it may make sense to hire a full time content editor or social media manager. If you just had one site, there probably wouldn't be sufficient work to retain them full time. Your internal processes and systems can also be shared across all the properties you own, making this a smart move the minute you have a competency with at least one site.

Business Model Changes

Whilst the emphasis in the previous examples have been on making an acquisition to complement what you already own, even a first time buy can be strategic.

I love examples - *you might have noticed*. Here's another:

Consider a blog for sale on asbestos removal - a service with a significant cost and lots of competing advertisers. The owner currently has an RPU of $0.05 from AdSense adverts placed on the blog.

You do some research and notice that there are several sites that appear in search results for the keyword 'asbestos removal'. They all seem to focus on capturing the visitor's details rather than serving adverts.

Most of them don't display a physical address or phone number, which is a good signal that this is an affiliate or aggregator. You call a few building companies to ask if they would buy leads, at which point you discover they would be prepared to pay up to $50 per confirmed lead.

In the site's current model, switching from **AdSense** to **Lead Generation** would mean you only have to convert 0.1% of visits to confirmed enquiries in order to improve the site's revenues. If the owner wanted a 4 - 5x multiple, you can justify this knowing that it's highly likely your changes will boost revenues overnight.

Arguably, this isn't a strategic play - it's more 'website acquisitions 101'. However in my opinion, having knowledge about what changes will and won't work is a strategic advantage that many buyers won't necessarily have pre-purchase.

Lifestyle Acquisitions

A purchase decision doesn't always have to be financially driven.

I've seen a few purchases made at significantly high multiples because the owner had a personal connection to the business or the niche that it was in.

For example, if you spent the last thirty years as a hobbyist stamp collector, and a stamp-collecting forum came up for sale, an acquisition makes perfect sense.

This is partly because you have the knowledge and expertise that another investor probably wouldn't have. Also, it's unlikely that anything you do in this business will feel like 'real work'. You see lots of advice about following your passion in business, but the reality is your passion is rarely what will scale or make you the living you need to run that business full time. If you're lucky enough to find a business that is your passion, then paying over the odds isn't the worst thing that you could do.

This decision isn't financially **driven**, but there's no reason that it can't make financial sense too despite being one you've made primarily for personal reasons.

If you enjoy travelling for example, then a travel blog could make perfect sense. This could be because of the freebies for your reviews, or because of the '*tax write-offs*' you'll inevitably notch up along the way whilst travelling anyway. After all, that luxury upgrade is totally a business expense and the overpriced masseuse was crucial in helping you write all those reviews …

The same rules apply for food, fashion, beauty or anything else that could be considered an expensive habit.

SUSTAINABLE MONTH ON MONTH GROWTH

We often joke about Silicon Valley valuations, usually in reference to any seller who wants a 10x annual net multiple for their six month old website. There is some logic behind why venture-backed valley start-ups often achieve ridiculously high valuations.

In some cases, it's because the acquisition is a strategic one. In layman's terms the acquiring company can extract more value from that acquisition than the average investor could, or in some cases the owners themselves.

In other situations, it's down to growth. Many Silicon Valley start-ups are SaaS, Mobile apps or Social driven applications. Their users will contribute to the company's profits so long as they're actively using the service.

Take those cases where there's a significant cost of switching to another service. With storage providers like **Dropbox** or marketplaces like **Uber** that have achieved critical mass, many of those users will use the service for years to come offering guaranteed revenue.

Providing that company continues to acquire new users at a greater rate than it loses existing ones, it should theoretically see consistent month on month growth. The value of the new users will add to the value from the existing ones, and profits in 12 or so months will be significantly higher than profits now.

This justifies a significantly higher valuation when looking at a smaller internet business purchases too. Take these two examples (*real examples from Centurica's Marketwatch, with the numbers rounded up to make calculation easier*).

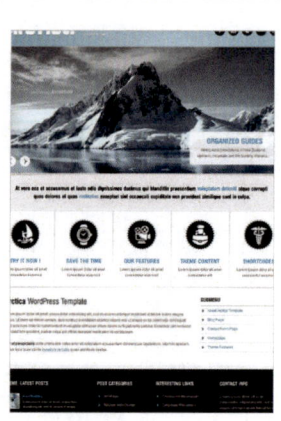

SITE A - TRAVEL AFFILIATE

Affiliate site that reviews package holidays to adrenaline filled locations.

Annual Revenue: $151,000 | **Annual Net:** $120,000

Asking Price: $240,000 | **Multiple:** 2x

Site A is a travel affiliate that sells package holidays to adrenaline filled and sometimes dangerous locations. (*Seriously, people pay good money to do this*).

It generates an average of **$10K per month** net ($120K per year) and is being sold at a valuation of 2x for **$240,000**. The site recruits visitors through PPC and each customer orders an average of 1.1 times in their 'lifespan', which means that it's unlikely they'll order again after their initial purchase.

SITE B - HOSTING AFFILIATE

Hosting review site focusing on cloud hosting, dedicated and virtual servers.

Annual Revenue: $37,000 | **Annual Net:** $33,000

Asking Price: $240,000 | **Multiple:** 7.27x

(*Annual Net based on Trailing 12 Months Profit*)

Site B is a Hosting Affiliate that receives monthly commissions on cloud based, dedicated and virtual server hosting. It generates an average of **$20 per client** each month they remain a hosting customer. It has a current client base of 250 clients.

Each month the site **gains an average of 27 additional clients** through PPC and loses an average of 7 from its existing client base. This is a net gain of around 20 new clients on average each month on top of what was there from the previous month. So for example, one month on they would have 270 clients, while the month after they would have 290 clients etc.

Because the site is growing continuously, the seller has extrapolated the most recent month's profit (250 * $20 = $5K) to work out the annual net figure. This is 12 * $5K = $60K per annum. At first glance, you can be forgiven for thinking the seller is insane, as their annual net profit should ideally be based on the last twelve months performance (*in this case it was approximately $33,000*).

Furthermore, he or she is asking for $240,000. Even using the seller's best case scenario, this is a 4x multiple and 7x if we use trailing twelve months net profit.

At first glance, Site A seems like a much better deal but let's see how much each business would be worth after a three year period. Assuming you make no changes or improvements to the site, and they continue to perform as is:

	Travel Site	Hosting Site
Current monthly net profit	$10,000	$5,000
Cumulative 3 year net profit	$360,000	$446,000
Value of site at 3x multiple based on trailing twelve months profit	3 * $120,000 = $360,000	3 * $221,000 = $663,000
Initial investment	$240,000	$240,000
Benefit	**$480,000**	**$869,000**

Even with the unlikely event that Site B would sell for as little as 3X TTM (*Trailing Twelve Months net profit*) in three years time, the investment is still worth almost double what Site A is in the same time period.

Spotting High Growth Acquisitions

The above example is an easy one to illustrate on paper, but in reality finding acquisitions with predictable growth isn't always easy. However, it's still not impossible. You can increase your chances by focusing on the following types of internet companies

- **SaaS Businesses** with scalable methods of user acquisition
- **Member Sites** and **Private Communities**
- **Affiliate sites** with a recurring commission – hosting is probably the best example
- **Mobile Applications** that have managed to achieve viral growth

Depending on the market or vertical, you'll also have to consider **decay** – the point where growth slows down or stops altogether, as no business can sustain growth indefinitely.

This is usually due to market saturation, increased competition as the market enters maturity, or inevitable issues with scale as the business begins to 'grow up'. There's no accurate way to forecast which, if any of these problems will occur whilst you own the business.

Given that you'll encounter them regardless of whether or not the site is a growing one, the benefits of a high growth acquisition still make it worthwhile.

101 :: PORTFOLIO STARS

08.
DO DILIGENCE

104 REDUCING RISK

108 THE DOMAIN

110 ONSITE CHECKS

112 TRAFFIC AND MARKETING

117 REVENUE SOURCES

120 BUSINESS MAINTENANCE

123 THE SELLER

REDUCING RISK

Remember I made the bold promise of showing you how to reduce your risk to a minimum? The solution is Due Diligence.

It's the closest thing you'll get to a silver bullet in this entire book.

For those of you who have bought or sold offline companies, Internet business due diligence (DD) requires a unique and very different outlook compared to a conventional business. Website DD is about looking at a website objectively through an established framework. Essentially, you're trying to find any misrepresentation or fraud on the part of the seller, but you're also looking for any factors that could potentially cause problems after you've made a purchase.

Have you experienced that feeling where you want to throw up at the thought of handing over $000,000s for a business you've just discovered?

Due Diligence makes most of that feeling go away.

The problems you typically avoid through thorough DD include

- Losing your traffic to a search update six months into owning the site.

- Finding out that the site's main source of revenue no longer exists or due to a policy violation, the site you own is no longer able to offer it.

- Realizing that the claimed revenue (which was backed up by a video walk-though) was in fact faked, or comprised of revenue from more than one site.

- Meeting your newest competitor that appeared several months after you bought the site only to find out it's the seller. What's worse is that the competing site provides many of your valuable backlinks that will soon be removed.

- Finding out you've spent three months negotiating with someone who doesn't own the site.

If you've ever made an auction purchase and the above list reads like a diary for you, this section will help ensure that none of these issues go overlooked again.

DIY or Outsourced Due Diligence

I'll start by disclosing that as a co-founder at a due diligence agency, I'm possibly the least impartial person to write this section. I'll try to keep the arguments relatively neutral so you can decide for yourself.

People tend to underestimate how much work goes into accurately assessing the risk of purchasing a site.

Someone who is experienced and good at performing DD will be able to guarantee more successes. They can see more failures that will inevitably happen – the ones that can't easily be fixed, and avoid the purchase altogether if necessary.

Tony Robbins tells the story of a factory foreman who had a power cut one night, and called an electrician to fix the problem. This factory stood to lose thousands if they were unable to resume work. The electrician arrived, turned a screw and the electric came back on. He billed the company $1,000 to which the foreman was less than impressed.

He was asked why he had charged so much for simply turning a screw. The electrician scribbled on an invoice:

Turning Screw	$1
Knowing which Screw to turn	$999

The foreman laughed and paid his bill.

I've probably screwed up some key points of that story. After all, no one can tell a story like Tony Robbins, but the point is the same.

Anybody can theoretically find the problems eventually, but someone who does DD on a regular basis is more likely to see it straight away. As professionals, we can take a look at a site and in a couple minutes tell that the traffic is spoofed and the entire site is a scam for example.

Alternatively, it might be something that's more subtle, like knowing exactly where to look to find that link that connects the seller to a competing site that they haven't disclosed. Something that you might be likely to miss unless you do this every day and use the same tools and software that costs several thousand each month to have access to.

It doesn't just come down to experience though; it's also about time.

A typical mid-range report will take between four – five hours for someone experienced, but can easily take 20+ for someone who isn't. If you have ample time to spare, then DIY might be an option. The reality is, you will always be able to leverage more value from your own time by either searching for new deals, or working on higher-level strategy for your existing or future purchases.

The next few sections will give you an overview of the due diligence process. Regardless of whether or not you choose to do it yourself, it's still important to have an understanding of how the process works. If anything, this will help you quickly disqualify potential deals that don't quite stack up, in order to save spending money on producing reports for sites that you ultimately reject.

PERFORMING DUE DILIGENCE

Due diligence on websites and internet businesses requires a slightly different skill set to that which would otherwise perform good DD on an offline business.

With an offline business, you typically purchase the entire business - in other words, the whole legal entity. That includes bank accounts, company assets and liabilities. You might also assume responsibility for any agreements belonging to it, such as leases, loans and contracts.

With a website or internet business sale you typically purchase the asset only. In this case, it's usually the source code, domain, electronic files and related properties. You tend to do this through a company that you already have set up.

This means less to investigate and verify in some respects but a lot more in others. You now have the task of verifying traffic from various sources and revenue from various accounts, in addition to a whole host of other checks. The skills needed to do good website due diligence can be taught, but they're very different to those needed to conduct DD for offline businesses.

To make the task easier, we (*Centurica*) tend to break due diligence down into six components:

- **The Domain**
- **On Site Factors**
- **Traffic and Marketing**
- **Revenue**
- **Maintenance**
- **The Seller**

Each component has its own set of checks and verifications that form a bigger picture as to how much risk is involved with your potential purchase. Website due diligence is possibly another book in itself, but I'll aim to give you a good foundation over the next few pages.

THE DOMAIN

Primary Goals

- **To establish who the true owner of the domain and most likely, the business is.**

- **To detect whether the business could have changed hands recently**

To perform these checks you will need a subscription to DomainTools.com or any other good WHOIS utility. I'll link to a selection of tools you can use for every part of this section in the book's downloadable resources.

Performing a check on the owner is relatively straightforward; you simply run the query and Domain Tools will give you the information it has. At this stage you're trying to establish if the person that you're communicating with is the person who owns the domain, and by association, the website.

Any good broker will often do this check for you, but it's an invaluable thing to do if you're buying something from a marketplace or direct from a seller. Even the best brokers still make mistakes though, so it's good to do this check regardless.

You'll also need to go back a few records to look for any changes in the sites' registrant, name server or IP details and piece that information together to work out the likelihood that the site was recently sold.

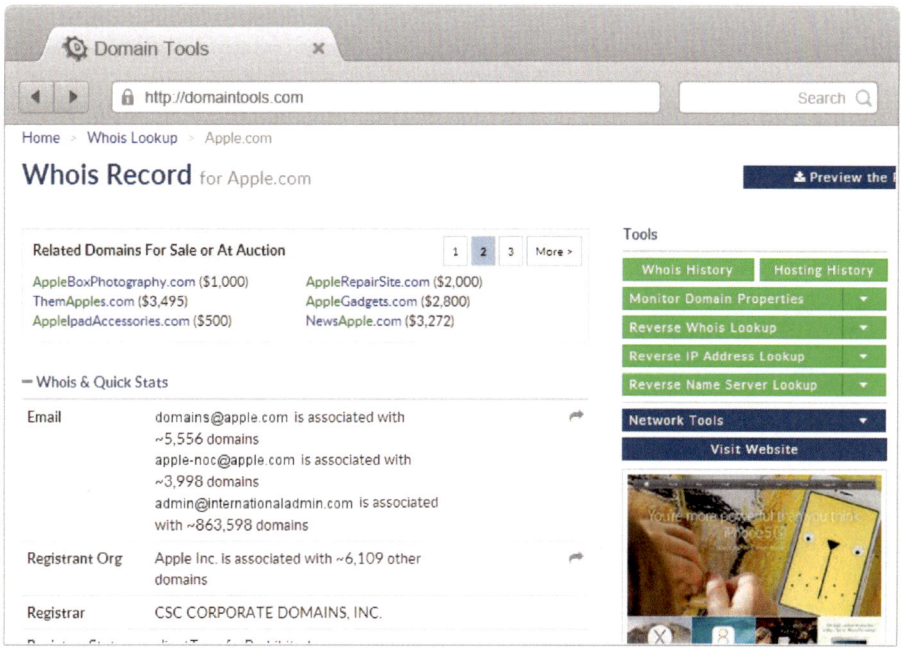

For example, if I can see that the registrant, name server and IP address of a site all changed six months ago for example, then there's a high chance the site changed hands at that time.

This is important to know, because a site that was only bought in the last year for example may have some hidden issues if the new owner is attempting to sell it already.

Further Checks

At this stage of your DD, you'll also want to discover

- If the site has had issues with spam or appears on any blacklists

- The true website age, which isn't always the domain's age. You'll need to look for historical records that show the site in its current incantation.

There are links in the resources pack to two free tools that will handle both of the above checks for you.

Primary Goals

- **Check the site's primary engagement metrics.**

- **Check for anything in direct violation of Google's quality guidelines**

When we measure engagement, we tend to look at a combination of pages viewed per visitor and the website's bounce rate. In isolation, neither of these metrics will guarantee that visitors are engaged. Both can easily be faked or inflated. We use them alongside the other information we gather to help us form a fuller picture.

You can calculate the average number of pages per visitor by taking the total page views (*now called 'sessions' in Google analytics*) per month, and dividing that by total visits (*aka 'users'*) for the same period.

For example, a site with 40,000 monthly page views and 19,000 unique visits has a PPV (pages per visitor) of:

$$40,000 / 19,000 = 2.1 \text{ pages per visitor}$$

This is a useful metric to know, as it can alert you to potential engagement problems if they exist.

For example, the industry average PPV for an ecommerce site is approximately 2 pages per visit. Given a margin of around **30%**, we know that a site with a PPV massively below this indicates that visitors possibly find the content 'thin' or poorly targeted.

Alternatively, a high number can be a sign of good engagement, in other words, visitors like the site enough to want to read more. An excessively high number however, can sometimes be a sign of traffic spoofing or the use of scripts designed to increase page views to deceive advertisers.

As with anything else in your due diligence, you can't take just this figure in isolation and expect a reliable result. It ideally needs to be compared to other similar sites in that niche to get a sense of whether it's normal or abnormal. Its real use is in helping us paint a picture along with the other data we look at, helping identify something that isn't quite right.

You'll also want to check the site against **Google's quality guidelines** – a checklist of 20 or so principles that determine their idea of a quality site.

This may not be so important if the site doesn't rely on Google traffic, but it's generally a good indication of a quality site. It also provides a list of areas to fix if you decide to make the purchase.

Further Checks

While you're investigating engagement and quality, it's also useful to check

- If the site uses cloned or scraped content, or has had its content copied by other websites.

- Whether there are any trademark issues associated with the site or the business behind it.

There are links to some free tools to help you do both of those in the downloadable resource pack that comes with this book.

Primary Goals

- **Spot unsustainable, fraudulent or low quality traffic sources**

- **Verify the traffic information supplied by the seller to ensure that it's accurate**

- **Predict likely drops in a site's traffic and often revenue too**

Most of your due diligence research will center on the website's traffic and marketing. This is the part of our own due diligence reports that take the most time to complete.

Traffic and marketing analysis is a vast subject that requires some experience to master. What we'll cover here are a few points that I think are important to know and will get you off to an adequate start.

One of the most important things to look for is how dependent a site is on various sources of traffic.

For example, people sometimes assume that organic traffic is priceless, because it's free and often converts well. When a site receives more than half of its visits from Google or Bing search, there's a high possibility that many of those visits could be easily taken away. A penalty, an algorithm update or even new competitors entering that market and pushing the site further down in the search results will all result in lost visits. If the site relies on new visits for revenue, for example to click adverts or to buy products, then lost visits equal lost revenue too.

Any site that receives more than 60% of its traffic from search is, in my opinion, a gamble because you have no control over that traffic and it could halve or even disappear overnight.

Another common issue is where a site receives the majority of its visits from direct or referral traffic.

There can sometimes be a logical explanation for direct traffic. Perhaps the business does a lot of offline advertising, or it's the kind of site with a short URL that people tend to type in directly. Providing you know that this is both sustainable and something you can control then having a lot of direct visits isn't too much of an issue. The problem is when we can't explain where the traffic comes from and as such we have no control over it. It could drop or disappear at any point and you would be powerless to do anything about it.

In the case of referral traffic, it's also a double-edged sword. If a blog receives 70% of its visits from hundreds of links on different respected, established blogs and portals then that's not a bad thing. The problem is when all of those referrals come from just a few sites or blogs or, as is most common, 80% comes from just one site. **The danger is that the link that drives the traffic could be removed at any time.** Worst still, the site may be owned by the same seller who will remove or redirect the link after the sale has completed.

You often see referral traffic problems with sites that rely on selling products through Internet Marketing Forums. A seller might do tens of thousands in revenue during the early months, but completely flat-line after that tiny forum market becomes saturated and the product fails to sell anywhere else. If you've purchased the business just after it's had its best month, then you're in for inevitable disappointment.

Similarly, imagine a site where the owner is frequently launching and receives most of their new customers from using other site's email lists. You have the inherent risk that you don't own or control any of those lists, so recreating that traffic as you, the person without all those relationships and strategic partnerships, is going to be difficult.

The key point to understand is that there are hidden dangers with nearly every traffic source. Your job at this point is to check how dependent the site is on each one, and have a good contingency in place should it ever run dry.

ANALYZING TRAFFIC SOURCES

ORGANIC SEARCH

While organic search traffic often converts well and is perceived as a relatively stable traffic source, it's important to understand that this type of traffic can be extremely unstable. This mostly because any changes in the search engine's algorithms, or an increase in competition can affect the website's rankings considerably.

Websites that rely heavily on search traffic are therefore at the mercy of the search engines, and this type of traffic should be considered as relatively high risk.

EMAIL

Email traffic tends to be relatively stable, providing that traffic can be attributed to a list owned by the site. Over time, email lists tend to become ineffective mostly due to attrition, so it's important that systems to continually grow the site's email list are in place and converting..

DIRECT TRAFFIC

Direct traffic (e.g. visitors typing in the address of the website directly or accessing the site from a bookmark) can originate from various places. The main ones are often untagged links in emails or word-of-mouth marketing. It's difficult to track the origin of direct traffic, so be cautious in situations where it represents a significant share of the site's overall traffic.

SOCIAL NETWORK

Organic Social Traffic (non-paid) should be treated in the same way as email traffic, where it's stable to the point that subscribers continue to grow and be engaged with.

REFERRALS

Referral traffic (e.g. visitors from links on other websites) can be relatively risky in nature, due to the fact that the sites in question can remove the links responsible for this traffic at any time. Also, referral traffic can often originate from (*disclosed or undisclosed*) paid for deals, which are unsustainable or short-term.

It's important to analyze the main sources of referral traffic and determine whether the sites in question are likely to be trustworthy sources long-term.

SOCIAL CONTENT

Traffic from content aggregation platforms like Medium or HubPages can be extremely unsustainable as the platform controls all of the traffic flow. If that platform happened to close, or there was a change in their rankings, then you would suffer a major decline in traffic.

Discovery sites like StumbleUpon also provide high volume but low quality traffic, that tends to convert poorly.

AFFILIATES

Affiliate traffic can be relatively stable, but it also comes with a number of risks and maintenance issues. Affiliates can require support, and the retention rate of affiliates is often low. This means needing to recruit new affiliates on an on-going basis.

In many cases a small number of affiliates bring in the majority traffic. Situations like this carry an extremely high risk, as a single affiliate who stops promoting the website will have a substantial impact on the business's overall traffic and revenue.

PAID TRAFFIC

Paid Traffic is a relatively safe and stable traffic source, as long as the seller includes all of the campaign details in the sale. In low-competition niches however, a new competitor competing for ad share can drastically increase your advertising costs.

Web Lies and Traffic Fakes

You'll also want to check that the traffic to the site is genuine. It's not uncommon for some unscrupulous sellers to spoof their traffic to either give impression that the site is doing better than it actually is, or to disguise fake purchases or clicks that they're making themselves.

Anybody can buy really cheap traffic.

5,000 "targeted" visitors will cost less than $25 and it usually comes from automated servers (bots) or pop-ups. Neither of these will ever convert to revenue. People are often surprised to learn that you can fool software like Google Analytics into thinking those visitors came from Google itself as organic search traffic.

When you analyze a site's traffic, here's what we recommend you do to avoid being caught out:

> **1)** Most analytics packages work by either analyzing log files on your server, or by asking you to run some external code on each page of your site. Never trust those that use server log files as your source of analytics. This includes programs like AwStats or Webalizer. Even JavaScript based programs like Google Analytics can be fooled, but it's much harder.
>
> Faking server stats simply requires changing a few files on the server and it's much more likely that the data you're seeing will be incorrect even without deliberate deception.
>
> **2)** If a seller claims to have a significant amount of organic traffic, do a reality check. Use a tool like the Moz Rank Tracker to see where they rank for the keywords that seem to deliver the majority of their traffic in the analytics report. You can take the software's traffic estimates to work out if the total traffic claimed by the site is realistic.
>
> The 80:20 rule applies here, where 80% of the site's organic traffic will usually come from the top 3 - 10 keywords. You'll only need to check a few keywords to get an idea.
>
> **3)** If you don't know what keywords the site ranks for (*it no longer shows in Google Analytics*) you can use keyword data from Bing, or even better, the site's Webmaster Tools account if they have one.

Primary Goals

- **Spot unsustainable, fraudulent or low quality revenue sources**

- **Verify the revenue data supplied to ensure it's accurate**

- **Look for issues that will come with transferring revenue accounts**

Just like with traffic sources, every source of revenue has its own qualities that determine how sustainable it is.

A site that relies on software sales from one specific forum for example, is unlikely to be sustainable. At some point, the market for that product will become saturated and sales will tail off. Advertising sold on a CPC basis however is much more sustainable, and will most likely generate income providing the site has traffic. The idea is to look at all the contributing sources of revenue, and establish:

- **Reliability**. How likely is it that this source could become unavailable.

- **Seasonality**. For example, textbook sales will peak at various times of year, so a three month average could be misleading.

- **Redundancy**. How easy it would be to replace.

You also need to consider how transferable a particular revenue account is. I'll give you a few examples. Some revenue accounts are easy to transfer and simply involve adding yourself as a new user and removing the seller, for example an Amazon Associates account.

Likewise, some accounts are not directly transferable but still easy to transfer. The best example is Google AdSense. You can't transfer the AdSense account unless it's registered to a company that you're also acquiring. You can however setup your own account to transfer the existing adverts into. You would and simply switch the AdSense ID over in the site's HTML, so clicks (*and hence payments*) are now credited to you.

It's not always this straightforward though.

A site that has several affiliate accounts will often be problematic to transfer especially if the new owner is from a different country to the seller. Many affiliate programs have fairly strict criteria and so it's not always guaranteed that you will be able to setup all the accounts that the previous seller had. Naturally, it's best to check this during your initial assessment and get a head start on any problem issues early on.

Another potential problem is when the site has recurring revenue from users setup in something like PayPal.

Unless you're taking over the business attached to the account, you can't transfer the entire PayPal account and you can't transfer individual subscriptions. This leaves you in a situation where you're forced to ask clients to re-subscribe – something that will inevitably lose a percentage of existing business.

Conducting a Live Screen Share

Your primary concern with revenue is to verify its accuracy and this is more difficult than verifying supplied traffic data. Although I mention 'revenue', I use this as a broad term to often include verifying costs too and hence profit, depending on how the business being sold operates.

When we verify revenue accounts for Centurica clients we tend to favor a live screen share. Here are a few tips to help you do your own.

1) Always start by checking the setup on the seller's machine.
You'll be viewing a live screen share and I'll share a few free tools to do this in the resource pack. It's good practice to start by checking that the seller doesn't have his or her machine configured to route to a spoofed version of one the sites that you're checking.

For example, I could setup a fake PayPal site on my local machine and configure the hosts file so that when I got to Paypal.com, I'm taken to my own local version that will show whatever I want it to. To check that this isn't the case, you should examine their hosts file before starting.

2) Watch them log into each revenue account progressively.
Don't be afraid to ask them to log out and log in again if you need them to.
I usually start with the ones that have the most data such as merchant accounts, as they usually queue reporting. This way, they can run the reports you need and check on another revenue account in a different tab and come back to that one when the report has been created.

3) Choose a snapshot of periods that give you good coverage of the information you're verifying.
In an ideal world, you'll check everything, but if your or the seller's time is finite, then it's probably a good idea to check the last full month, the last full year and another two months that you've selected at random and check the totals agree with the data you've been supplied.

4) Be careful with PayPal.
There's no solid way of telling exactly what site a sale originated from, but you can examine details on randomly picked transactions to get an idea of who the buyers were and where they were located.

BUSINESS MAINTENANCE

Primary Goals

- **Establish the time and tasks required to maintain the site**

- **Look for tasks that require a specific skill, or alternatively can be outsourced**

- **Estimate the costs likely to be involved with running the business**

As far as misrepresentation goes, this is a part of your DD that's also highly likely to flag up issues. In fact, owners understate the amount of time it takes to manage and run their business in the majority of sales we see.

Unless you're craving the opportunity to purchase a job, and mostly likely a poorly paid one at that, dedicate time to getting this part right.

Before looking at maintenance, it's important to make the distinction between **Owner time** and **Resourced time.**

Imagine a blog that publishes technology related articles and generates revenue from advertising. The business has three writers and a part time editor who checks and posts their content. The site is advertised as '*Fully outsourced and automated earning $1,250 net per month*'. You figure the business is a steal at $20,000.

Let's assume the owner has correctly included costs for those writers and the editor on their income and expenses (profit and loss) statement. We can put these tasks to one side for now as these aren't our primary concern. This is what we refer to as **Resourced time**.

Our main concern is any work the owner puts in, or any work performed by someone else that hasn't been financially accounted for. In the above example, this could include, but isn't limited to:

- Doing enough SEO or link building to maintain the site's current traffic levels.

- Content outreach, guest posting and social media updates - again, just enough to keep pace with what was previously been done.

- Site maintenance

- Dealing with advertisers

- Content planning and marketing calendars

All of these tasks could easily add up to 25 hours per week if done right.

Suddenly, what you considered to be a passive income bargain, has become a part time job earning approximately $1250 / (25 * 4.3) = **$11.63** per hour. Worst still, you've had the privilege of paying $20,000 for it with no chance of a refund.

Another area where misrepresentation occurs is in operating costs. There are no fool-proof ways of accurately verifying every one of the seller's claimed costs. You can usually verify the majority of them and fill in any blanks with comparative costs and common sense.

Here are a few guidelines when verifying maintenance costs. To be clear, these are overheads and not cost of goods sold.

> **1)** A good way of looking at this is to imagine that you're creating the list of overheads from scratch. You're using what you've been supplied with by the seller as a guide, but not as an accurate rendition. This is where having some knowledge of the business and its required tasks will come in useful. If in doubt, a professional due diligence agency or buy-side broker should be able to help.

2) Using what the seller has supplied as a basis, begin to list out all the overheads that are associated with maintaining the current level of business.

The idea here is that you're looking at maintenance and not growth. So for example, if the seller currently has a PPC campaign running and this generates customers who order just once, then you'll need to continue that campaign to recruit new customers and generate that income each month. This is a maintenance expense, or in fact two. The cost of the clicks and the cost of the time in having you, or someone else to manage the campaign.

On the flipside, if the site being sold is an app for example, there will be fixed costs associated with developing the product that you'll never have to pay again. You will need to allow for upgrades, new features and bug fixes but these are likely to be a fraction of the initial development costs.

3) Brainstorm likely overheads that may not show up on the seller's expenses statement, but are likely to occur while you own the business. This will most likely include software expenses (*licence renewals for tools and plugins*), software development and upgrades for applications.

4) Go back to each item you've listed and enter a sensible monthly cost next to it. In some cases, you can use what the seller has supplied, but now is a good time to get a reality check on whether those costs are in line with what you would expect to pay. If in doubt, get a quote by placing a job on somewhere like Elance or Guru for outsourced tasks or lookup software expenses or hosting costs on the sites from which they originate.

Your goal is build a list of expenses independent of what you've been supplied, to answer the question of whether the costs you've been supplied are accurate.

This process has frequently seen the claimed profit of sites reduced by more than 40%. When sellers realize they have omitted a significant amount of cost, they're forced to recalculate their selling price.

Usually, being thorough in this process can save you thousands if not more.

THE SELLER

Primary Goals

- **Find out if the seller owns any relevant other sites they've not disclosed.**

- **Discover any previous and related sales by the same seller.**

Undisclosed sites that the seller hasn't mentioned could pose a threat for three reasons.

1) Once the seller has sold the business, there's every chance they could **develop that undisclosed site into a competitor**, assuming it's in the same niche.

2) The undisclosed site might be **referring a substantial amount of traffic** to the site that you're purchasing. This will cause a problem if the seller decides to sell that site or redirect the traffic elsewhere after you've taken ownership of the business for sale.

3) The undisclosed site might contain **backlinks** to the site you're purchasing. If the seller decides to remove those links after the purchase, this could affect your search rankings.

Often, a seller can genuinely forget to include a site they maybe started some time ago, but haven't since had a chance to maintain. In this case, prompting them to include it in the sale may be all you need.

On the other hand, I've seen situations where sellers deliberately haven't disclosed URLs or sites they own because they intend to keep operating them as a separate and competing business.

What you do at this stage is entirely up to you, but personally I would give the seller the ultimatum of including it in the sale or walking away from the deal. The deception would also put me on high alert about everything else that has been supplied so far.

09.
CREATING DEALS

129 SELLER FINANCING

132 HOLDBACKS

135 EARNOUTS

136 EQUITY RETENTION

CREATING DEALS

The common misconception from new buyers is that a deal is accepted or refused solely based on the offer price meeting the seller's criteria, but that's far from the whole truth.

Every seller has a walk away number – an amount that makes sense to them which is most likely not the number the business has been listed at, even if they don't know this yet. On average, according to data published by BizBuySell, the **average brokered business sells for around 89% of its asking price**.

On a $500,000 business, that's **$55,000** to be saved just by submitting the correct offer.

I don't know how reflective this statistic is for the industry as a whole, but a broker colleague of mine recently mentioned that less than half of the buyers he deals with makes an offer that's even 5% less than the asking price. Some never negotiate at all, which means a lot of money gets left on the table.

Simply calling up brokers and low balling isn't (always) going to work though. Sellers tend to accept lower offers when there is the absence of certain factors and the presence of others. Knowing these ahead of time and positioning yourself correctly will always work in your favor to earn you the best deal.

Speed
Every seller, no matter how much they feed you the generic *"I'm not in a rush to sell"* line appreciates someone who can complete a transaction quickly. Personally, I always make it clear to the seller or broker that I know what I'm doing and have no issues completing this deal quickly because:

- I know what I want and I'm confident to purchase providing the site passes DD.

- My DD will be done by professionals and that process will take very little time providing I have their co-operation.

- I have the funds ready as cash in the bank and the transfer will arrive into Escrow within the day once initiated.

Remember the experiment that involves offering people $5 right now or $10 in ten months?

The majority of people will take the $5 for instant gratification and the certainty of the offer being fulfilled. When a seller can see the end of deal is just around the corner, they will often prefer that offer even if it's not the highest one on the table.

Credibility

Being able to convince a seller or broker that you're both legit and committed goes a long way towards positioning yourself to being a more attractive prospect to do business with. The internet allows everyone to be as anonymous as they decide to be, but coming out of the shadows and allowing a seller to get to know you will work in your advantage.

It might be a little brash to drop the *"Do you know who I am? I'm kind of a big deal"* line into your first conversation. A more subtle variant can work just as well.

During your email communication be sure to include links to your social profiles (Linked In, Facebook, and Twitter) and any business you might currently own or work with, to give the reassurance that you're a real person who is less likely to disappear mid negotiation.

Remember, this isn't a job application. If your Facebook profile isn't squeaky clean (*and you've been tagged into more than a few Jaggerbomb moments at 3am*), don't worry. Most sellers or brokers are looking for evidence that you're a real person with a high likelihood of going through with the deal.

Not being an Asshole

It's surprising how much of a difference being likeable makes and more surprising how many people 'forget' to be nice.

Having played both the buyer, the seller and on one occasion, the broker, I've always been far more likely to offer concessions to a buyer I like, who I know will look after the business and appreciate the deal.

Put yourself in the shoes of a typical buyer. You've dedicated a large chunk of your life to building something that you now have to sell. As well as the financial difference that comes from selling the site, you're also concerned about what will happen to an entity many people will still associate with you personally, years after you've made the sale. If the site includes a community or a regular audience, then you feel even more responsible for ensuring standards are maintained and those users keep receiving value.

If you had the choice between a corporate entity paying $200K and a solo entrepreneur paying $180K, it's highly unlikely your personal preference for the entrepreneur will swing the sale, regardless of how much you like him or her. Narrow that gap down to $200K and $195K respectively, and having a connection with the seller could easily swing the sale in the entrepreneur's favor.

People will always prefer to do business with those who they like. Believe it or not being likeable, creating rapport and asking for a discount because it's all you have, will go a long way towards getting one.

Being able to transact quickly, appearing credible and being a nice person to do business with, will all contribute to getting a better deal on a purchase. The real magic happens when you find creative ways to structure that deal.

Common Deal Structures

Unlike buying an offline company, an internet business or website purchase is typically an asset acquisition – not a business sale. This is an important concept to understand and often comes as a shock to new buyers used to conducting transactions in the offline world.

Unless otherwise stated in the sale agreement, you typically purchase the domain, the website files such as code or images, any databases and mailing lists and the rights to any transferable social media properties or related sites and domains.

You don't purchase the entity (*the business*) behind the site, nor do you acquire any of their assets (*cash, equipment etc*) or liabilities (*debts, leases, loans*). This for example, is also why a major part of our due diligence is focused on how transferable a particular revenue source is. It's unlikely it will be transferred as part of the sale. Another example where this is relevant is with staff. The majority of websites being sold use outsourced or contracted staff rather than employees. It's often assumed that those contractors will continue to work for the website, but it's not a mandatory term of sale.

In my experience, around **40%** of sellers are looking for a straight cash sale (no terms) and would never be prepared to entertain anything else. The remainder are often open to reasonable suggestions, even if they haven't realized it yet.

There are four common deal structures that could all work in your advantage as a buyer which we'll cover in a little more depth.

SELLER FINANCING

Bank financing was a common way to part fund the purchase of traditional businesses prior to the financial crisis. After bank lending tightened up, buyers had to find more creative ways to finance a deal. **Seller financing** was one way to solve that problem.

The seller accepts part of the sale price in installments over a defined period of time. More recently, seller financed deals are becoming commonplace in Internet Business transactions too.

As a buyer, the main benefit is leverage. You can achieve a greater return on the same amount of capital invested versus a deal with no financing available. Whilst it's common in the offline world for the seller to charge a substantially higher selling price when they're financing part of the deal, that isn't the norm with website sales. Sellers are often happy with a nominal increase and / or a reasonable amount of interest and in some cases, no interest at all (*although those deals seem to be much harder to find lately*).

From a seller's perspective, they have two benefits. The first is being able to potentially receive more for a business when finance is made available. If the seller isn't in a hurry for the cash, this can mean outstanding returns from an average site.

Also, sellers have the benefit of being able to quickly sell a site that may have otherwise sat unsold. By offering finance, you widen your market to include more buyers, some who may not previously have been able to afford the site.

Avoid making the common mistake of asking for seller financing as a way to protect you against potential downside by keeping the seller 'invested'. There are better ways to achieve the same thing, which we'll cover further on. If something were to happen within the business, you would still be legally responsible for the debt (without other provisions), making financing unsuitable as a means of buyer protection.

A basic example of financing

The premise of seller financing (SF) is simple; you pay a lump sum upfront and the remainder over a set period of time, usually 6 months to 2 years. With bricks and mortar business sales, it's common to have some collateral to secure the debt against, but strangely it's not that common with internet business sales.

For example, if a web business is valued at **$800K**, you might pay **$400K** on completion of the deal and the remaining **$400K** in quarterly payments over the next 2 years (*i.e. $50K each quarter*). From an investment standpoint, because you've purchased $800K worth of business with $400K worth of capital, and get to keep all of the website's returns from the moment you take over.

3 YEAR ROI ASSUMING A SALE AT THE SAME PRICE THE SITE WAS PURCHASED FOR:

(($800,000 + (2 x $160,000)+$360,000) - $400,000) / $400,000 = 270% ROI

3 YEAR ROI ASSUMING A SALE AT THE SAME PRICE THE SITE WAS PURCHASED FOR:

(($800,000 + (3 x $360,000)) - $800,000) / $800,000 = 135% ROI

Assuming that business generates approximately $360K of annual net profit (before payments to the seller), then you're not only paying directly out of the company's profits, but you're also going to have a sizeable sum left over each quarter too.

This is the ideal financing situation for buying a web business, as it allows you to leverage your capital and grow a portfolio rapidly without using mainstream finance. Naturally, this works best if you reinvest all of your profits into more purchases.

Here's the caveat; those 'perfect' deals have become harder to find and most sellers now charge a premium or interest, even if it is a relatively small sum. In some cases, I've seen asking prices jump by 20% when finance is an option.

Assuming the $800K price tag from our previous example is the 'listed' price, this is usually based on the assumption that the deal is done as all cash. In other words, everything is paid on completion. The price would most likely be north of $800K if finance was an option. In addition to, or sometimes instead of a slighter higher selling price, the seller may choose to charge interest (*typically between 6 and 12%*) on the financed portion of the deal.

Our $800K deal example is being sold at a 2.2x annual net multiple; relatively low even for an 'average' site of this size. If the seller decides to charge 8% interest on the $400K financed, the numbers change slightly. You'll ultimately pay around **$64,087** in interest over two years making your total purchase price **$864,087 – a multiple of 2.4x annual net**. If the interest figure were to increase to 14%, your total purchase price would be nearer to **$912,153**.

Weighing up Risk and Opportunity

The two examples above look at an interest rate of 8% and 14%, but what if the seller asked for 20% or 25% instead? There are a number of calculations you can make that will each bring you to different conclusions about whether or not this investment would be worthwhile.

Looking at the cost of interest doesn't factor in your potential return over 3 or 5 years on an $800K business versus going for a $400K deal with no financing bought as cash. Being able to purchase a business with $30K monthly net, as opposed to $15K monthly for a website that's half the price, will inevitably return more despite the fact it costs more to purchase overall. This is the effect of leveraging your investment – in my experience, one of the fastest ways to grow.

You may also have other alternatives and more creative ways to finance a portion of the deal. For example, if a seller asks for 20% interest, you might be able to fund part of the deal through an SBA loan or credit card advance at less than 20%. It makes sense to finance as much as possible through that method first, before using the seller to fill the remaining gap in your finance requirements.

HOLDBACKS

As a buyer, you typically ask for a holdback when there's some uncertainty about the business's future performance.

Holdbacks are probably the most difficult deal to negotiate as from a buyer's point of view, they offer less money upfront with no real upside. In many cases, people sell because the potential gain from having the business doesn't outweigh the risks associated with keeping it. In these situations, a holdback is highly unlikely with a seller who wants to make a clean break.

A holdback will (should) usually be held in Escrow for a specific period of time and released when clearly defined conditions have been met. In some cases, it could be a short-term holdback like one that's dependent on the outcome of a pending legal case. A situation I recently encountered had a holdback of 5% that was contingent on an app the business submitted being accepted into both the Android and iOS app store. Most holdbacks are more long term in nature and tend to be because of the following scenarios.

Expiring Agreements

The business has agreements or contracts in place (with either suppliers or customers) that could expire soon, without any guarantee of them being renewed. Usually, the business will need these agreements to continue to operate at its current performance.

This is common with content sites that rely on advertising from private advertisers that is renewed annually or biannually. The chances are, some of those contracts will expire within months of you purchasing the business. To this day, I'm yet to speak to a seller who isn't 130% confident their advertisers will renew post sale. Naturally, this doesn't always happen.
Implementing a holdback clause based on a percentage of revenue over the next 12 – 24 months will give you some of the guarantees you need.

The Pareto Dilemma

With any business that relies on strategic partners or affiliates, it's highly likely that they'll follow the Pareto principle. 80% of the company's revenue will come from just 20% of those partners. There's an interesting theory that this repeats itself. Of that 'prize' 20%, 80% of the revenue will come from 20% of that particular group and so on.

Losing just one of those partners can have a huge impact on your bottom line. Sellers will often try to appease you by stating how long these partners have worked with the business and how it's in their best interest to continue the relationship. Things can change drastically when the personal relationship between the seller and that partner no longer exists.

Suggesting a holdback to guarantee revenue from those key partners, will usually help balance the risk that they could easily stop promoting or worst still, start to work for your (better paying) competition.

Declining Traffic and Sales

Last year, a colleague asked me to speak to a broker on his behalf about a site he was considering purchasing. Below is a transcript of part of the conversation that was recorded for his benefit as he was unable to listen in on the call live.

When you've spent long enough speaking to sellers and brokers, you'll hopefully laugh and relate to the following scenario. *Those of you familiar with the industry may even be able to guess who the broker was.*

> **Myself:** "So the one main concern I have now I've looked at all the revenue data directly from Ultracart [*shopping cart software*], is that sales seem to be declining month on month since August last year. If [*removed*] was buying the business as a distressed asset, then this conversation would be irrelevant, but the valuation you're asking for is higher than some businesses I can buy right now, that have no obvious issues. Do you have any thoughts on this?"
>
> **Broker:** "What do you mean. Traffic has been going up since way before then and continues to rise even this month?"
>
> **Myself:** "Yes. And that's amazing, but revenue has been going down."

> **… awkward pause, followed by what sounds like the broker covering the mouthpiece and asking someone a question**
>
> **Broker:** "We've spoken to the client about this and I can promise you it's not a problem. This business relies on listing inventory… you know … staying current. These women go crazy for the latest [….. *removed for privacy*] but it has to be new stuff. The seller hasn't been able to add new inventory as he's been busy with another project so sales have fallen off. With all the new traffic, it's almost guaranteed that if you add inventory, sales will return back to their normal level. Actually, it will be way past its normal level because the new normal is booming"
>
> **… my awkward pause, while I digest what "***the new normal is booming***" actually means.**

I asked the broker if the seller would consider a holdback for a percentage of the asking price.

This would be based on the new owner adding a specified amount of new inventory at or above previous levels. The broker's reaction to this suggestion was a good indication that he wasn't the only one who didn't believe his claims that revenue would easily return to normal.

If you've found the perfect purchase but you're concerned about declining traffic or revenue that the seller is convinced will return, then a holdback allows you to offset some of the risk, but also tests that seller's confidence in their claims.

This works the other way around too. If you've spotted a business with a recent and rapid growth curve, or one that's just acquired a lucrative new client, some sellers may want to value it based on trailing six (or even three) months profit. Use a holdback to give you some protection in the event that growth spurt is short-lived, especially if you happen to be paying a premium for it.

EARN-OUTS

In many ways, an earn-out is identical to a holdback – you retain some of the purchase price and pay out when a condition is met, but often an earn-out will have some upside for the seller and usually allows them to directly influence the outcome. This makes it an easier deal to accept, as there's some tangible benefit to the seller by saying yes.

Take this example.

You're negotiating on a SaaS business that offers project management and billing software to freelance web developers. The owner previously did some impressive deals that brought on several $1,000s in additional revenue from just a handful of strategic partners. She's convinced that there's scope to do much more of this and projects that profit will double in the next year.

Assuming an asking price of **$200K**, and an annual net profit of **$50K**, an earn-out could take one of a couple variations.

1) Business performance based earn-out
You pay $150K upfront, and 25% of profits over the next two years. If the business remains at the same level you'll pay $200K (*which according to the seller is highly unlikely to happen*). If the business loses sales, you'll pay less and if it continues to grow as the seller has promised, you'll pay more. If growth were to double to $100K per year, then the total that seller would receive is $150K + $50K + $50K = $250K – a $50K increase on her asking price, making this something highly worth considering.

2) Seller performance based earn-out
You offer the same deal as 1) above, but the seller continues to work generating new business for the site. This way they're directly in control of the amount of additional revenue they generate with no limit on the upside. This is typical where the seller performs a sales function for their business such as business development or advertising sales.

As an earn-out is far more likely to be accepted than a hold back, I'll often lead with a suggestion of a hold-back to test the water, but then defer to an earn-out when that suggestion is rejected. As a rule, use holdbacks to protect against negative situations that the previous owner would have no control over once they sell the site. Use earn-outs as a way to profit from a confident seller, or a promised upside that the seller will be able to control or deliver after they've made the sale.

EQUITY RETENTION

If a seller believes in the long-term success of their website under your new management, you might be able to trade part of the payment for equity in the new company you've formed to acquire the site.

As an example, you might offer **$300K** for a **$400K** site on the condition that the seller retains **25%** equity in the new company you've formed to purchase their site. If you decide to sell a number of years later having grown the business and realized its full potential, then the previous seller can still share some of that upside.

Part equity deals tend to be common with larger sites that have enough potential to achieve substantial growth, but are in some way stunted by the current seller and their management. This could be due to focus, lack of capital or inexperience.

A similar idea is to merge their business into your existing established company.

You offer a smaller share of your business, assuming it's a larger company that roughly equates to the non-cash part of the purchase agreement. So if your existing business is valued at **$1,000,000**, using the example above you could offer **$200K** as cash and the remaining **$200K** as a **20%** share in your company allowing them to benefit from the synergy that the two businesses merging will enjoy.

It's not uncommon for the previous owner to take a non-exec or advisory role in the acquiring company. In some cases, it can also be a paid one depending on the depth of their involvement.

10.
EVERYONE NEEDS A PRENUP

141 GOOD INTENTIONS

143 DECONSTRUCTING YOUR PURCHASE AGREEMENT

146 WAIT ... I ACTUALLY NEED A PURCHASE AGREEMENT?

148 ADDITIONAL CONSIDERATIONS

151 ESCROW AND DEPOSITS

Up until this point, you've navigated **hundreds of bad sites** to find a website that truly is a **value investment**.

You've overcome disappointment when you realized that one in a million business has been **sold**.

You've started the process over again and **found another gem**. You've gone through **due diligence**, analyzed every detail with a fine toothcomb and decided that any **shortcomings** are ones that you can live with.

You've **structured the perfect deal** and the seller has signed off.

If you've come this far, you're a glutton for punishment. Somewhere, there's an outstanding return waiting for you that makes it all worthwhile, but there's one final hurdle to overcome.

In this section, we dissect the purchase process and look at the agreements and processes you undergo to complete the deal.

GOOD INTENTIONS

Chronologically, this section probably should have been a couple chapters back. Just after you make an offer, the broker, or perhaps the seller, will issue a Letter of Intent (LOI).

It's typically a one to two page document that outlines the terms of the offer and sets the foundations for the **Purchase Agreement**, which is negotiated and signed later.

An LOI is usually prepared by the broker and sent to all parties involved as soon as an offer is accepted by the seller. It's signed by the buyer, the seller and in some cases the broker too. It's important to know that the Letter of Intent is **not usually a legally binding document**, but you should always verify this. It does set out important provisions for the Purchase Agreement and as such, should be reviewed as carefully as you would the main agreement itself.

There are a few important points to bear in mind when reviewing your LOI.

The Offer
You want to ensure that everything agreed verbally has made it into the LOI. The LOI should state all terms of your offer, including the purchase price, any holdbacks, earn-outs and any other conditions you might have agreed upon.

Wording
Is the wording in the document clear and not overly legal?

The sanity check that I like to perform is "would an unrelated person who happens to read the document have a clear understanding of what the seller and buyer has agreed on". Remember your LOI and Purchase Agreement have two very different purposes. While the Purchase Agreement needs to be legally binding, the LOI simply needs to be clear so both parties understand the terms they are about to proceed under.

Closing Deadline

An important part of the LOI is specifying a closing deadline.

This is the date that the transaction is expected to complete. This clause often goes overlooked, but it's important to pay good attention to it and not agree with an unreasonably short (*or an unreasonably long*) time frame. There should be sufficient time for both due diligence and the transfer process, as well as for the actual transfer of funds through Escrow.

Potential Legal Consequences

While an LOI isn't usually a legally binding document, you might notice a clause that is worded similar to

> *"This agreement is not legally binding to either party, with the exception of clauses X, Y and Z"*

If you happen to spot this, it's crucial that you review the clauses referenced that are legally binding. Ideally, you should run them by a lawyer to get a full understanding of the restrictions or liabilities that they potentially create.

Exclusivity Period

During the exclusivity period, the broker or seller cannot entertain any other offers. This means you can conduct your due diligence without fear that someone else will put in a better offer in the interim and purchase the business.

The length of the exclusivity period varies greatly from one agreement to another. Some brokers don't include this clause, but in most cases it falls between one week and two months, depending on the size of the acquisition.

DECONSTRUCTING YOUR PURCHASE AGREEMENT

You should always seek legal advice before signing a Purchase Agreement. If you're not planning on using a purchase agreement for a deal, fast forward to the next section for a little insight.

Some agreements are fairly straightforward template documents while others are long and complicated. Interestingly, it's the more simple agreements that often cause issues, as it's easy for the other party to include a one-sided set of terms that go overlooked.

Before sending your agreement for legal review, it's worth saving your attorney's time and your money by doing as much of the review as you can yourself. Here's a brief guide to navigating a typical website purchase agreement.

Inclusion of Covenants
Purchase agreements often render any communication or agreements made prior to its creation null and void. This can include your original **Letter of Intent**. It's important to make sure that absolutely everything that you've agreed on with the other party has been included.

Inclusion of Materials
In some cases, the other party may have provided you with materials that you were basing your offer or valuation on. You need to ensure that all of those materials are added into the Purchase Agreement as appendixes and referenced in the agreement itself.

These materials can include anything from due diligence documentation, to copies of agreements signed with suppliers or with staff. In the event that they're not included in the purchase agreement, it's likely you'll have to take lengthy legal action if they happen to be inaccurate or falsified.

It's also a good idea to have the seller warrant the truthfulness and accuracy of any materials added to the agreement.

Imagine a situation where $100,000 of revenue is claimed on an income statement sent to you by the broker facilitating the deal. It later turns out that this was a misrepresentation and you decide to sue the seller. After consulting your attorney, she gives you the bad news. No income claims were made by the seller, it was all from the broker. **As the broker isn't a party in the agreement you have no claim and therefore you have no case.**

Warranties

Even if the seller warrants that everything they have told you over email is true and accurate, make sure that these warranties extend to the broker, if there's one involved.

Deal Structure

As with the LOI, you want to make sure that everything that you've previously agreed has made it into the agreement. This extends to any holdbacks, earn-outs or timed payments. They should all be clearly explained and impossible to misinterpret.

It's also wise to check that the agreement clearly defines the timeline of the transaction. Both you and the seller should be crystal clear about when and how funds and assets are to be transferred, whether you're using an escrow service and under what conditions funds should be released to the seller.

If one of the parties in the agreement is a broker, then you need to also make sure that it's clear who is liable for broker fees. It's most likely the seller, but if by some odd agreement it happens to be you (…*sucker*), be clear as to what the fees amount to.

Misrepresentations and Termination

Assume that all of the materials provided in the due diligence phase have been attached to the agreement and the other party warrants that the materials are true and accurate. This will be of little help if misrepresentations aren't considered grounds for termination.

You need to make sure there's a clause that clearly allows you to terminate the agreement if the seller breaks any of their warranties. It's also wise to specify that you should be reimbursed any funds already paid.

References to Included Assets

Everything included in the sale should be clearly referenced in the contract. For example, if there's a Facebook page included in the sale, make sure that the contract is worded along the lines of *"Facebook page names 'ABC' with the web address 'http://XYZ'"*, rather than *"Facebook page related to the website"*.

Professional Help

It always pays to consult legal counsel prior to signing an agreement. In addition, you should also seek assistance from an independent industry professional, to make sure that everything is in order.

An attorney can decipher fine print and vague clauses, but they're likely to miss industry-specific aspects of the contract, unless they specialize in online acquisitions. You can usually find buy-side brokers via an online search (*naturally, not the broker representing the seller in the transaction*).

My own biased recommendation for help and advice in this area is Centurica.com.

Non-Compete

A non-compete clause will prevent the seller from competing with the business that's being sold. It's up to the buyer and the seller to negotiate the terms of the non-compete, such as its range and duration. As far as online businesses are concerned, where barriers to entry are relatively low, signing a non-compete is considered the norm.

If the seller is for some reason unwilling to sign a non-compete then pay close attention to their reasoning behind it. Often enough, this kind of unwillingness is a red flag on its own.

Jurisdiction

Something that often goes unnoticed is the jurisdiction (country or state) that governs your agreement.

This is probably the first thing that you should check when first drafting the agreement, or reading through it if it's drafted by someone else. The jurisdiction effectively determines the country and state in which you need to seek legal counsel.

It's probably not a wise idea to run a contract past your US attorney if the contract jurisdiction is for example, England. The laws in England or in fact any EU Country, are entirely different from those that apply in the US.

Similarly, there are many legislative differences across the US states, meaning that if at all possible, you should look at hiring an attorney in the same state that governs the agreement.

Wait … do I actually need a purchase agreement?

We occasionally speak to buyers who think preparing and signing a Purchase Agreement is largely a waste of time. In their mind, it serves no real purpose, especially if they use an escrow service for the transaction.

If you like gambling, playing roulette offers more fun and better odds than relying on escrow alone to keep you protected during a deal. Whether you're the buyer or the seller, having a good purchase agreement drafted and signed by both parties can potentially save you from bankruptcy.

There are a few reasons why having a good purchase agreement is often a lifesaver.

Escrow comes with no warranties
The primary reason for signing a purchase agreement rather than relying on Escrow is that most escrow services for online transactions won't allow you to define warranties. As long as the seller transfers the assets the transaction is considered completed and funds are released to the seller. In most cases for an internet business, this is just the domain name and the website's code.

This leaves you vulnerable when there's a problem with the assets that you've received. For example, if the code that you've been sent is incomplete, or not what is currently being used on the site.

Alternatively, you may have been sent all the site files, but none of the customer information or mailing lists. The seller could decide they want to continue to market to these people from their new business. As far as the escrow company is concerned, you've received everything that you're entitled to, and the seller will be in the clear.

Protection in the case of misrepresentation
More often than not, escrow services also provide little protection against misrepresentation.

Imagine a scenario where the seller claims a business is generating $10K per month. You buy the business (forgetting to do your DD fully), and discover that it's actually making half that amount. You go back to information that was previously provided by the seller and realize that it has been forged.

A good purchase agreement will allow you to take the seller to the court and reverse the deal, but without one, you're out of luck. An escrow service only looks at whether you received the asset or not, rather than whether the characteristics of the asset had been misrepresented.

Claims that arise after the asset transfer
Escrow will only protect you until the point at which the site has been transferred, but not afterwards. The majority of issues arise only after the site has been transferred. Often, it's several months after. This is mostly down to the time it takes for you as a brand new owner to become acquainted with the business and see the full picture.

Having a watertight purchase agreement offers some protection in the event of a fatal problem arising several months into your ownership.

Having a structure for resolving disputes
In your Escrow service's terms and conditions, you'll usually find the fine print that defines exactly how disputes are resolved. Unsurprisingly, those terms are often borderline evil. If most people fully read and understood their implications, it's highly unlikely that they would ever voluntarily agree to them.

It's in the escrow provider's best interest to resolve all disputes as quickly and efficiently as possible, even if it means that the resolution might not be fair. You'll usually find a list of pre-selected arbitration courts where you have to take your case to. Even if you wanted to, you couldn't sue the other party in a 'real' court as you surrendered that right when you signed the escrow agreement.

Naturally, having a purchase agreement in place takes this problem away. If drafted correctly, it should supersede any terms and conditions imposed by the escrow firm.

ADDITIONAL CONSIDERATIONS

There are standard terms that you're likely to find in any purchase agreement, but sometimes these fail to give you all the protection that you need. You'll often need to add separate clauses that contain conditions or stipulations specific to the type of asset that you're about to acquire.

With so many different types of business available for sale, it's difficult to anticipate and advise on every possible variation to look out for, but you'll find a few common issues that frequently appear.

Honoring Old Agreements

With any business that has a recurring revenue element, it's usually wise to check if the seller has any customers signed on a long-term agreement. Aged agreements can be problematic in two ways:

1) Draining Resources
Around two years ago, I spent some time with a seller who had a SaaS business that allowed designers to create online portfolios to showcase their work.

At the time of sale, the seller 'forgot' to disclose around 60 users he had taken on at a price which was a quarter of the existing subscription. Those users were all part of a design college, and the college had signed an agreement that had three years left to run.

The nature of the service was that users required more storage and bandwidth the longer they were with the service. They would always add new content like large graphic files or videos, but never remove it, because there was no limit on their account. The cost of servicing those 60 users was only marginally profitable when the site was being sold, but it was estimated that in around 6 months each user would result in a loss, if they continued to add content at the same rate.

Technically the sale was an asset purchase, not a business purchase. If I did buy the business, I could easily claim that the agreement was made with the previous company and increase prices, but ethics aside, this wouldn't be a wise idea. The bad sentiment and word of mouth would most likely do more damage to the company than allowing those users to finish out their plan.

When you draft your purchase agreement (or even the LOI), be very clear about what previous agreements and contracts exist with current customers. While you don't have a legal obligation to honor them, you most likely have to factor the cost of doing so in.

2) Presells
It's common for sellers with membership sites to have pre-sold lifetime subscriptions to early signups. This isn't usually a problem when you're simply delivering content, as the additional bandwidth to serve those users is often minimal.

The problem is when those users have access to support, advice or as I've seen in some cases, one to one mentoring or consulting with the owner. The only thing that can add insult to the injury of buying a business and discovering you have hundreds of free accounts to support, is knowing that the revenue they paid to make that possible will never go to you. The fact you'll have to service those customers is something that you probably expected to do, but many people are unaware of the fact that they will never be paid for these users.

Just as in the previous example, the problem isn't so much the legality, but the bad sentiment this causes especially in community-focused sites. Ask the seller to disclose any pre-sells upfront, and work out a plan to minimize the drain on resources going forward once you own the site.

Maintenance Plans

You experience a change in mindset the moment you decide to sell a business you've worked on for any length of time. At first, it's subtle. You convince yourself that you're still **100%** committed, but the reality is, it's more like **90%**.

Once you start to receive concrete offers, that **90%** becomes **70%**. Sign an LOI with a genuine buyer and the average seller is now down to around **50%**.

To be clear, not every seller intentionally lets things go post sale. In fact, it's usually unintentional if it does happen at all, but it does happen. The longer your due diligence, purchase agreement and transfer process takes the more damage is potentially done. This can range from simple issues like running low on stock and not leaving enough time for a new shipment to arrive, through to letting customer support emails go unanswered for an unacceptable period of time.

It's usually wise to agree a minimum standard with the seller that you expect to be maintained up until the point where you take ownership. This can cover, but shouldn't be limited to

- **Minimum levels of stock to maintain.** The seller should be responsible for reorders until the point where you take over.

- **How and why customers should be emailed.** It's not uncommon for less ethical sellers to exhaust their mailing list in an attempt to squeeze additional sales prior to the transfer. This is gives them a boost in revenue that they inevitably keep, leaving you with problems and a poorly performing list when you take over.

- **Continuing any advertising** that's active when you first discovered the site. This is more common when there's a relatively long sales cycle. Some sellers cut back on advertising, or stop entirely. The seller is usually responsible for the bill up until the point you take over, so in their eyes, they probably won't see any benefit and will still have to pay out. Without it though, it will inevitably affect what you have in the 'funnel' when you take over.

- **Continuing to post content and update social media** at the same rate as when you first discovered the site. The most sensible option is to take a three months average and use this as a benchmark for a minimum.

- **Maximum response times** for customer support tickets or emails. It's easy to let non sales emails build up especially when you know they'll shortly be someone else's problem.

With the exception of extreme circumstances, failing to stick to your agreed maintenance plan is rarely grounds to terminate the entire deal. You can impose financial penalties, providing they're pre-agreed and very clear. In some respects, the maintenance plan is a bluff.

The benefit in having it is mostly to show the seller that you've quantified what's important to the business. It makes it very clear that you intend to act if you fail to take receipt in the condition it was when you originally agreed to purchase.

ESCROW AND DEPOSITS

Once you've agreed on the terms laid out in the purchase agreement, it's common to transfer the purchase amount into Escrow.

If you've never used a digital escrow service before, they simply hold your funds and release them to the seller once they've transferred the domain and the website's files. As we discovered earlier on in this section, that's far from being an ideal solution, but it offers more security than simply transferring your funds to a seller and waiting in hope for everything to arrive.

In some cases, the broker might have asked you to pay a deposit of approximately 10% when you signed the LOI. This tends to be more common if you're a newer buyer or you've never conducted a transaction with that seller before. Some smaller brokers use this as a way to guarantee their fee, taking this as their upfront payment. Naturally, if you've already paid a deposit, the amount you will deposit into Escrow will be the purchase price minus the deposit amount.

If the transaction is just between you and the seller, then the Escrow company will usually act as the 'referee'. You initiate the transaction and send the funds directly to them, and they notify the seller once those funds have cleared. The seller then initiates the transfer of their domain and the site files.

Once you've received and are happy with everything, you notify the escrow company and they make the payout to the seller. If the transaction involves a broker, they will often be the referee, and notify the Escrow company when either side has an update.

Escrow fees are typically 0.8% - 1% and these are usually split between you and the seller.

11.
AFTER THE HONEYMOON

154 THE PERFECT TRANSFER

162 A VIEW FROM 30,000 FEET

170 BUILDING A PORTFOLIO

AFTER THE HONEYMOON

The most technically challenging part of the process for new and experienced buyers alike is the transfer stage.

Without a combination of experience and planning, what should be a painless process that happens over a couple of days, can turn into a drawn-out two month ordeal. Apart from burning valuable time for both you and the seller, dragging the process out will naturally result in loss of income for your brand new business and could seriously affect your reputation with users.

There's no such thing as a standard transfer. Every site has its own moving parts and idiosyncrasies that make transferring it along with its domains, social accounts and other related properties unique.

The following guide is a set of best practices that have been developed mostly through trial and a whole lot of error on several business acquisitions. If you lack technical skills, or don't have a technical person on your team it would be wise to hire one to do the bulk of the work for you. When you acquire a new site, the odds are always against you, and an outage or screw-up will do little to help.

The Perfect Transfer

It's important to understand that there's a difference between a '*transfer*' as defined by the escrow company and a transfer which we we'll shortly dissect.

Your escrow company will usually pay when assets have been electronically transferred. This means

    1) You have ownership of the domain name and

    2) You've take possession of the site's files.

What could go wrong huh?

A full transfer process typically involves:

- Ensuring the site is setup on your server, or taking possession of the seller's existing one.

- Checking that all of your subdomains, checkout urls and secure urls are working

- Checking that all of the email addresses previously setup still work and now route to or are accessible by you

- Updating the contact and billing details for all the accounts you've taken ownership of.

- Checking you now have ownership of ALL of the seller's related sites and domains

- Ensuring you have access to every third party social property, marketing service and shopping cart

- Ensuring that your account is the one receiving payment for products sold or ad revenue generated.

With the list of things that could potentially go wrong in mind, you should ask the seller to complete as much of the transfer process as possible. Ideally, you'll get them to do this before you transfer your funds out of escrow.

If you are faced with managing the process yourself, the following guide should help.

Step 1 - Creating a transfer list

Start by creating a list of every asset to be transferred in a spreadsheet. I usually split this into three tabs.

Tab A - Domains and Sites
As well as being able to keep track of the transfer of each domain, you also want to know how everything is set up, as those settings will often be lost when that domain moves registrar. This involves knowing which domains are linked to sites, where those sites are hosted and how much traffic that site receives. This is useful when you have a lot of domains to identify smaller sites that might not be worth while keeping or setting up again if the hosting isn't part of the deal.

Tab B - Accounts
Regardless of whether or not an account can be or is being transferred, it's a good idea to list every third party account the business uses in one place.

THE PERFECT TRANSFER
AN OVERVIEW

01. Create a Transfer List

Start by listing out all the accounts, assets and contacts to be transferred.

02. Account Setup

Begin to apply for all the accounts you'll need to operate the site. Do this early, as merchant and other financial accounts often take extra time to come through.

03. Hosting

At some point, you'll need to decide whether you should move hosting to a new account you've setup, or alternatively transfer the seller's existing hosting account.

04. Make Code Changes

Assuming you'll be setting up some accounts from scratch rather than transferring the seller's into your name, you'll need to make updates to parts of the site.

05. Account Updates

For the accounts that are being transferred, work through each one connected to the website and update the billing or payment details as you go.

06. Stock

If you're purchasing an internet business with stock, ask the seller to do an inventory and get ahead on what will need to be reordered.

07. Warm Introductions

Ask for an introduction to the key people involved in the running of the business.

This way you can track details that need to be updated and logins that need to be transferred. It's crucial that you include every account necessary for the operation of the business and that will extend to:

- Hosting accounts being transferred with the business.

- Marketing Accounts like email marketing software (e.g. Mailchimp, Aweber), CRM and marketing automation software (e.g. InfusionSoft, Salesforce) and Advertising Platforms like Adwords or Bing Ads.

- Analytics Accounts such as Google Analytics or KissMetrics

- Commerce Platforms that include shopping carts, marketplaces, seller accounts (e.g. Amazon or Ebay) and fulfillment center logins. This also includes mobile app marketplace accounts that sell an application included with the sale.

- Bank, Merchant and Revenue Generating Accounts such as PayPal, Google AdSense or Clickbank.

- On Site Plugins and Helpers such as Helpdesk Software (e.g. Zendesk), or live chat plugins.

Tab C - Contacts

Depending on what the business does, it's likely you'll need contact information for a variety of key people that will include:

- Key suppliers and manufacturers

- Contractors and Outsourced Staff

- Affiliate Network Contacts

- Strategic Partners and High Volume Affiliates

- Moderators, Super-users and Volunteers

Naturally, you should have a personal introduction by phone or email to everyone who matters, but it's always a good idea to have the seller confirm their contact details for your records.

Step 2 - Getting a head start on account setup

You can use the list you just created as a basis for knowing which accounts you'll need to create yourself. For example, it's unlikely that you'll take the merchant account with the site, so you'll need to setup your own with the same provider and swap your details out.

You would be shocked at how many times buyers leave setting up a merchant account until a few days before they take over a new purchase.

They soon realize their merchant account will take several weeks to be approved and now they have no way of taking customer payments. In reality, most sellers will continue to process the payments on your behalf but it's not something you want to rely on. Accounts that typically have setup delays include

- **All revenue accounts** – for example PayPal, merchant accounts and naturally bank accounts.

- **Affiliate accounts**, especially if you reside in a different country to the network or seller.

- **Supplier credit accounts**. If the business relies on obtaining goods on credit from a supplier, ensure you've either left ample time, or you have cash available to pay for inventory.

Running this process as early as possible gives you a critical head start on ensuring a smooth handover.

Step 3 - Setting up hosting

At some point, you'll need to decide whether you should move hosting to a new account you've setup, or alternatively transfer the seller's existing hosting account. In my experience, **it's almost always a better idea to initially take over the existing account.**

The goal of a good transfer is to reduce the number of potential points of failure. The less we change the less likelihood that something will go wrong and if it does, it's more likely you'll be able to isolate and fix the problem. This means putting off any unnecessary changes that don't need to be made right away until the business has been transferred to a point where all the relevant dangers are under your control.

If you can avoid transferring hosting, then do so as it's almost always a more complex job than you can imagine unless you're an experienced server admin. The seller can often update the payment details and contact details on their hosting account to yours, and send you the username and password.
In the event the seller has multiple sites in the same account, or cannot transfer the whole account for another reason, ensure you

- Transfer every database related to the site

- Configure any custom modules required at a server level

- Reconfigure the email accounts, assuming the emails are not hosted elsewhere. If they are, you may also need to reconfigure your new host or domain registrar to send emails to your hosted mail service.

- Update DNS entries. This is to ensure something like shop.mydomain.com still works post transfer.

Step 4 - Code updates

Assuming you'll be setting up some accounts from scratch rather than transferring the seller's into your name, you'll need to make updates to parts of the site.

This might be changing the Google Analytics ID, or inserting your own ad server code to ensure any ad revenue goes to you and not the seller post transfer. Wherever possible, ask the seller if they can make code updates on your behalf. Besides the fact they'll probably know the code far better than you do, any problems or errors that arise from their changes will be their responsibility to fix.

Step 5 - Payment, billing and bank account changes

Got through the list of third party properties on your transfer sheet, and work through each one, updating the billing or payment details as you go. If you've taken over the seller's shopping cart service such as Ultracart or Shopify, this will mean updating the merchant account and possibly PayPal details to your own. In the case of affiliate accounts or marketplaces, it can mean updating the payment and contact details so any funds are deposited directly to your account.

It's likely that there will be some overlap based on each service having different billing dates. You can calculate any pre-handover revenue minus any pre-handover costs and pay this to the seller in the month following the acquisition.

Step 6 - Ecommerce stock

With most ecommerce businesses that hold stock, it's likely that you'll agree to pay for it at value. The amount of stock will continually change as customer orders are sent out, so it's impossible to agree a figure for any stock upfront. The most reasonable method is to pay for the cost price of that stock on the date you officially handover.

It's a good idea to ask the seller from the start of the process what they estimate their rate of stock turnover to be for the store's more popular items. You can combine this with the supplier's lead time to establish when you will next have to place an order. This can be crucial to know ahead of time if that point arises while you're still conducting the transfer.

Step 7 - Supplier and key person introductions

Request an introduction to the key people that you listed on your transfer sheet. Rather than wait until a crisis happens (for example you run out of stock, a moderator becomes inactive or sales from a particular partner dry up), you'll have an opportunity to build a personal bond. This is done in the hope that they'll continue to deliver the same quality of work they did for the previous owner.

Post Sale Support

It's common for a seller to offer some form of post-sale support, but without a holdback or earn-out you shouldn't put too much faith in the quality or availability of the seller's help.

In my experience, sellers are always helpful, but at the point you need help the most they'll have most likely moved onto another project and resent being pulled back to their old one that they're now trying to forget.

Try to obtain all the information you will need before the transfer process is complete and before your money is released to the seller. Naturally, getting paid is the best motivation for most sellers and knowing that it hinges on them providing prompt answers makes it the ideal time to ask for their help.

A VIEW FROM 30,000 FEET

After writing this book, I took the advice of an outstanding author. He destroyed the original draft because there was too much theory, too soon.

This final chapter is all theory, but it's well deserved after many pages of practical advice. I believe that the people who have a grasp on the theory as well as the practical elements of any pursuit will always be those in the top percentile. This goes for anything be it sports, education, learning a new language or business.

The goal is to give you a higher level understanding of what makes a purchase right for you in your circumstances and what to do once you've acquired it. This will set you apart from the majority of buyers who do this process blind. They think buying cheap and doing more SEO will save them. Each individual purchase you make should be governed by the ideas laid out below.

You can succeed without them, but following them will greatly increase your chances of profitability on each deal. Their purpose is to make your job easier by going with the natural flow of what's likely to happen rather than working against it.

For every purchase I've seen that doesn't fail as a result of bad due diligence, it's usually because of a lack of understanding of these rules. These individuals usually go out of business, or give up when they make little to no progress and can't work out why.

When you make a new purchase you tend to land in one of two camps - **Development** or **Operational**.

The Operational Play

An operational play is best used on a website where:

- The business (*not just the domain*) has been established for longer than three years, and is usually perceived as an authority or established brand within its niche.

- It holds a significant share of its market. In most cases, especially with content or sites that rely on advertising, market share will be measured by unique visitors and page views and compared against publicly available information for competing sites within the same niche or vertical.

- It has an above average amount of revenue per user for its niche. This usually demonstrates good product market fit, where the site has found good products or adverts that match what its audience is looking for.

- It also has a sustainable and scalable system for customer acquisition. This would usually involve paid traffic such as adverts in search or on social networks.

This strategy is about purchasing low-risk, medium-low return assets, typically in the valuation band of 2.5x – 4x annual net profits. In other words, relatively expensive, older businesses with lots of history and average returns, but a low chance of failure and lots of things in place to safeguard its traffic and revenue.

These types of sites provide consistent, stable cash-flow over the time you own them and some appreciation in capital value, making this the cash-cow of any balanced portfolio.

How to achieve maximum returns

Once you acquire the site, your strategy should generally include:

1. Prioritizing defense rather than growth

When an older and more developed website has gained enough market share, it's usually a sign of either a growing or relatively mature market. If you choose an operational play as your strategy, then your selection criteria should ignore any internet business with a limited market size.

We can assume that you'll be operating in a large growing or mature market, which will inevitably mean frequent new competitors. In addition to choosing a business with sufficient barriers to entry, you should prioritize a strategy focused on defending your current position before you start to make plans for growth.

This might mean

- **Investing in Organic SEO** and content outreach from high-authority sites in the same niche as your new acquisition. Organic traffic converts well and is difficult for competitors to replicate. Assuming you already have an established paid traffic campaign, focusing on organic acquisition now will mean you can lower your cost to acquire one new customer far below that of any new competitors.

- **Creating differentiation** through design and a premium user experience. Customers may originally come on the strength of your content and marketing, but they tend to remember and recommend your site because it stands out and provides a good user experience. If you happen to be in a niche filled with me-too sites and blogs, investing in good design will increase retention and viral promotion.

- **Investing in software and systems** to make daily operations easier and more cost effective. For example, a new CRM system for a lead generation site to increase sold lead quality and to deliver it quicker and more efficiently than your competition.

2. Grouping certain tasks to minimize your overheads.

Assuming you have a portfolio with more than one Operational site, you should hire and train a centralized team. Even with just one site, you can often make savings through bringing certain functions in-house, assuming there is enough volume to make it worthwhile.

This can be your own in-house team or alternatively, a team of freelancers you've found via a marketplace like Odesk or Elance. The idea is **horizontal integration** – reducing your fixed costs and overheads by having the same specialist work on multiple sites handling tasks like Content Creation, Social Media, Paid Traffic Management or Front and Back End Development. This will always provide a cost saving versus the 'sum of parts' approach of hiring and training ad-hoc freelancers for each site, or retaining the individual staff that previously worked for the business.

You also have the added benefit of an increase in the quality of the work being done due to specialism. Single sites will typically outsource or multi-skill roles that don't require full time input (like development work or search marketing), but the synergy of having multiple sites using the same facility, often means a consistent output and higher quality of work delivered by your trained internal team.

3. Monetizing the entire customer funnel.
A mature site is highly likely to have adequately monetized a visitor or customer on their first contact with the site. After several years of operating a business, most (*sensible*) owners figure out the best way to convert a cold visit to a profitable click or sale.

The opportunity usually exists to develop monetization further down the customer funnel. This will usually involve investing in tools and software to segment, qualify and market different products and services to the existing customer base.

For example, a new owner of a property investing membership site could mine its existing email list and segment this into prospects, low-value prospects, higher value buyers and lapsed memberships. Using marketing automation tools like InfusionSoft, they could begin to market different products to each segment.

4. Acquiring smaller related websites.
Knowing the lifetime or long-term value of a visitor that fits the site's demographic profile will make smaller strategic purchases highly profitable. For example, if your current acquisition makes $50 from each visitor interested in organic diets through the sale of books and DVDs, then a smaller blog with the same audience that makes $10 from affiliate referrals or adverts would be a great purchase at the right price.

What to expect with an Operational Play

Your primary aim with an Operational Play is to **maintain, or increase its cash-flow**.

Any growth in the site's value is unlikely to be significant, especially if the website was purchased at a premium. Also, an exit before at least three years of ownership will rarely make sense, with five years or more being a sensible timeframe.

The Development Play

A development play makes sense on a relatively under-developed site that loosely matches the following criteria:

- It either has a high RPU (*revenue per user*) and low levels of traffic or relatively high levels of traffic and a low RPU. RPU will always be relative to other sites receiving the same demographic and quality of traffic, but not necessarily in the same niche.

  For example, a health and beauty site that attracts working moms might share the same demographic as a fashion site that showcases affordable work wear for women in their 30s. The RPUs of these sites could be compared as they are effectively monetizing the same audience.

- It holds little market share relative to the total market size.

- It has an RPU and average keyword cost per click that demonstrates a paid traffic campaign would be sustainable, but the owner has not yet implemented one.

- It has possibly struggled with achieving product market fit, or it has a good product or service that's simply wrong for the audience.

- It has not yet monetized 'further down the funnel'. In most cases, this means there is only single-user contact. For example, a user turns up and may or may not click an advert. There is then little or no attempt to capture that user's information and market to them on another occasion.

- It has traffic in a lucrative niche, but has not monetized that traffic to generate sufficient revenue or

- It relies on a single source of monetization like contextual advertising.

The Development Play is all about the acquisition of medium-high risk, high-return assets, typically in the valuation band of 1.5x – 2.5x annual net profits.

This strategy is about being rewarded for taking a risk, but you should still try to mitigate some of it upfront. To reduce some of the risks before you buy, your own criteria and due diligence checks should prevent you from buying:

- Sites that are less than one year old or receive less than 1,000 monthly visits.
- Sites that rely heavily on one source of new customers, usually outside of your control. This could be organic traffic, forum traffic, or short-term affiliate promotions.
- Sites that are built around a 'red-light' business model (see chapter 5)
- Sites that rely on unproven or unstable sources of revenue, or a new untested product.
- Sites that operate in a red-light niche or a market with limited size or potential.

The website you purchase might initially provide little to no cash-flow, but it will usually show a substantial increase once your development work starts.

As well as seeing growth in the amount of income the business generates, we're also looking for extreme growth in its capital value, eventually transitioning into an Operational Play for you or someone else if you decide to sell.

This would initially be the 'question mark' of your portfolio.

How to achieve maximum returns

1. Develop the amount of revenue earned per user.
The RPU of sites with similar demographics should give you a benchmark to assess how well developed this particular site is. You can also see what growth you can expect possibly through improving conversions, or changing its monetization strategy.

This typically involves

- **Conversion rate optimization** on the site's key landing pages

- **Implementing lead capture** and where (*financially*) possible, running retargeting campaigns, to sell to or generate impressions from otherwise lost opportunities

- **Exploring different monetization options** through modeling sites that achieve a higher RPU with the same type of traffic

You might see a business for sale that appeals to the same demographic as the site you own, but its RPU is twice as high as yours. There's no harm in requesting further information to see what they're doing right in terms of the types of monetization they use and their timing and placement for each.

2. Prioritize growth rather than defense.
Assuming the asset has relatively little traffic or market-share, your focus should initially be on growth followed by exploring new sources of traffic. This would involve:

- **Setting up paid traffic campaigns** where it's financially viable to do so.

- **Growing organic traffic** by investing heavily in high-quality content to appear on the site itself, related blogs and publications within the niche and on relevant social media channels.

- **Creating engagement** through social media, and connecting with industry influencers ahead of connecting with individual users.

- Exploring the feasibility of **recruiting users through other platforms** such as mobile, desktop software, plugins or apps.

- Working on **creating strategic partnerships,** syndications or affiliate relationships with other companies in your niche

3. Establishing and refining your Customer Lifetime Value.
If you've decided to use paid traffic, getting an idea for the lifetime value of each customer will help you create a strategy to improve it.

One way would be to look at the site's current portfolio of products, services or advertisers and examine where customer needs exist, but are not being adequately met. Introducing new products and services to fill this gap would inevitably mean more customer spend and hence a higher CLTV.

What to expect with a Development Play

Your goal with a Development Play is to transition into an Operational Play that will deliver stable on-going Cash Flow.

Growth in the value of the site itself is usually significant. In some cases, where the risk of owning that business is high (e.g. technology sites, trending products), it can make sense to look at a short term flip, selling the asset within 1 – 3 years.

PORTFOLIO DEVELOPMENT

You can easily generate income for yourself which is more than sufficient to live off without ever owning more than one site.

In fact, my advice for potential buyers who simply want an income that's more involved than property or stocks and shares, but less demanding than their previous job or business is to buy an Operational Site and simply hold onto it.

If you're looking to create 7 – 9 figure wealth that far surpasses what you would create from any other asset class, then you'll most likely need to trade several times. In other words, you would be selling to realize the value you've built up in one site and putting that capital to work in a bigger one. This is all on the assumption that you you're not starting with a 7 – 9 figure investment to begin with.

If you want to do this quickly, then you'll need to acquire and operate several sites and take advantage of the benefits of owning a portfolio.

Assuming your goal is to create 'above average wealth', you will ideally have a portfolio that

- Balances sites held for capital growth against ones held for cash flow.

- Creates an opportunity for operational specialism by purchasing businesses within similar niches, verticals or business models.

- Balances stable, mature, low-growth sites against riskier high-growth ones.

- Consistently generates a positive net cash-flow across all of your purchases, after all debt equity (e.g. seller financing or bank & SBA loans) have been serviced.

Building a huge portfolio is difficult, especially as managing multiple businesses involves a discipline in management that isn't required when managing just a few small sites.

The main benefits in running an internet business (no staff to manage, location independence) seem to be lost when running a large portfolio of sites. Somewhere in between a small hobby site and world domination is a happy number.

Large enough to deliver relatively big profits but small enough to avoid the headache of running a large business.

I'll tell you if I ever find out what that number is.

Made in the USA
Columbia, SC
13 June 2017